PIRKE AVOT

THE SAYINGS OF THE JEWISH FATHERS,
TRANSLATED WITH AN INTRODUCTION AND
NOTES

JOSEPH I. GORFINKLE

ALICIA EDITIONS

CONTENTS

PREFACE	1
INTRODUCTION	2
NAME	2
PURPOSE	3
DESCRIPTION	4
CONTENTS	5
LANGUAGE	6
DEVELOPMENT OF ABOT	6
ABOT IN THE LITURGY	9
BIBLIOGRAPHY	10

SAYINGS OF THE FATHERS

CHAPTER 1	17
CHAPTER 2	25
CHAPTER 3	35
CHAPTER 4	46
CHAPTER 5	56
CHAPTER 6	68

Notwithstanding the fact that there are many editions of the *Sayings of the Jewish Fathers*, and that it has been translated innumerable times in all modern tongues, no apology need be given for the appearance of this little volume in the series of *Jewish Classics*. The *Pirke Abot*[1] is indeed a classical bit of that ancient Jewish classic, the *Mishnah*.

The translation in this edition is based largely upon that of Taylor, in his *Sayings of the Jewish Fathers*, and upon the excellent version of Singer, in his *Authorized Daily Prayer Book*.

This edition is intended mainly for popular reading, but it has been thought wise to amplify the notes, especially with bibliographical references, so that it may serve the purpose of a teacher's handbook, and also be useful as a text-book for the higher grades of religious schools and for study circles. The references are to books that are generally accessible, and, wherever possible, to books in English. The notes are by no means intended to be exhaustive, but rather to be suggestive.

It is the humble hope of the editor that this little book may be the means of further popularizing the practical and, at the same time, high-minded wisdom of the "Fathers"; that it may serve as an incentive to a more detailed study of their philosophy of life, and that its appearance may help us to lead in a revival of that most ancient and praiseworthy custom of reading the *Pirke Abot* in the house of worship on the Sabbath, during the summer months. Let him into whose hands these sayings fall "meditate upon them day and night," for "he who would be saintly must fulfil the dicta of the Fathers."

JOSEPH I GORFINKLE.
Mt. Vernon, N. Y.
February, 1913.

---

1. We find both spellings, *Avot* or *Abot*. In Hebrew, the word אבות (which means "fathers" or "ancestors") can be transliterated either way, but *Avot* is more widely used today. *Editor's note.*

INTRODUCTION

NAME

The Tractate Abot (*Massechet Abot*) is the ninth treatise of *The Order* or *Series on Damages* (*Seder Nezikin*), which is the fourth section of the *Mishnah*[1]. It is commonly known in Hebrew as *Pirke Abot, The Chapters of the Fathers*, and has also been termed *Mishnat ha-Chasidim, Instruction for the Pious*, because of the Rabbinic saying, "He who wishes to be pious, let him practise the teachings of *Abot*"[2]. On account of the nature of its contents, it is generally designated in English as the *Ethics of the Fathers*. Taylor entitles his edition *Dibre Aboth ha-Olam*, Sayings of the Fathers of the World, and has as the English title, *Sayings of the Jewish Fathers*. Gustav Gottheil refers to the *Abot* as the *Sayings of the Pharisaic Fathers*[3]. Its German title is generally *Die Spruche der Vater*, and in French it is usually rendered *Chapitres* or *Maximes des Peres*.

---

1. See *infra*, n. 61.
2. *Baba Kamma*, 30a. See Taylor, *Sayings of the Jewish Fathers*, p. 3. Maimonides refers to this saying in the *Foreword* of his *Eight Chapters*; see Gorfinkle, *The Eight Chapters*, etc., p. 34.
3. See *Sun and Shield*, p. 321 *et passim*. See *infra*, n. 8, which accounts for the use of "Pharisaic."

The use of the word *Abot* (fathers), in the title, is of very ancient date. We can only guess at the reason for its being used, and, consequently, there are various explanations for it. Samuel de Uceda, in his collective commentary, says that as this tractate of the *Mishnah* contains the advice and good counsel, which, for the most part, come from a father, the Rabbis mentioned in it adopt the role of "fathers," and are therefore so designated. This explanation does not, however, deter him from advancing another to the effect that this treatise is the basis of all subsequent ethical and moral teachings and doctrines, and the Rabbis are, in consequence, the "fathers" or prototypes of all ethical teachers and moralists[4]. Loeb attributes its use to the fact that the Rabbis of *Abot* are the "fathers" or "ancestors of Rabbinic Judaism"[5]. Hoffman states that the word *abot* means "teachers of tradition" (*Traditionslehrer*), and points to the expression *abot ha-olam* (*Eduyot*, I. 4), which, translated literally, is "fathers of the world," but is used to designate the most distinguished teachers, which is a true characterization of the Rabbis of *Abot*[6]. Taylor says in regard to the title, "It takes its name from the fact that it consists to a great extent of the maxims of the Jewish Fathers whose names are mentioned in the pages"[7]. Hoffmann's seems the most acceptable explanation.

PURPOSE

The original aim of *Abot* was to show the divine source and authority of the traditional law revealed to Moses on Mt. Sinai, and to demonstrate its continuity from Moses through Joshua, the elders, and the men of the Great Synagogue, down to those Rabbis who lived during the period between 200 B.C.E. to 200 C.E. Loeb maintains that *Abot*

---

4. *Midrash Shemuel* (ed. Warsaw, 1876), p. 6. The *Midrash Shemuel* is a collective commentary, first published in Venice in 1579, and which has since passed through six editions. See p. 22, n. 21.
5. *La Chaine*, etc., p. 307, n. 1.
6. See Hoffman, *Seder Nesikin, Introd.*, p. xx, and p. 258, n. 36. In this passage of *Eduyot*, Hillel and Shammai are referred to as *abot ha-olam*; in *Yerushalmi Shekalim*, III, 47b, Rabbi and Ishmael and Rabbi Akiba, and in *Yerushalmi Chagigah*, II, 77d, all the pairs of *Abot* I are similarly designated.
7. Taylor, *loc. cit.*

was originally a composition of the Pharisaic Rabbis who wished to indicate that the traditions held and expounded by them, and which the Sadducees repudiated, were divine and, in time and sequence, uninterruptedly authoritative[8]. This line of continuous tradition is plainly seen in the first two chapters. A second and probably later purpose was to present a body of practical maxims and aphorisms for the daily guidance of the people.

DESCRIPTION

The *Sayings of the Jewish Fathers* is the oldest collection of ethical dicta of the Rabbis of the *Mishnah*[9]. It is a Rabbinic anthology. It has

---

8. *La Chaine*, etc. The Sadducees belonged to the priestly and aristocratic families. They made light of the oral traditions, did not believe in the future life, and were indifferent to the independence of the Jewish nation. The Pharisees, on the other hand, were constituted largely from the common people; they were believers in, and strict observers of, the traditional laws, and were ardent nationalists. The bitter attack of Jesus on them, which has resulted in making the word "Pharisee" synonymous with "hypocrite" and "self-righteous person," was, to say the least, unjust, as Herford has so lucidly pointed out in his sympathetic study of the Pharisees. Herford, though not a Jew, has taken up the cudgels most ably in defence of this sect, with remarkable insight into the life and literature of the ancient Jews. He demonstrates conclusively that though there were hypocrites among the Pharisees, as among all classes and creeds, yet the average Pharisee was a man of the most elevated religious ideals, who misunderstood Jesus, but who, in turn was misunderstood by him. Huxley, in his *Evolution of Theology*, says, "of all the strange ironies in history, perhaps the strangest is that 'Pharisee' is current as a term of reproach among the theological descendants of that sect of Nazarenes who, without the martyr spirit of those primitive Puritans, would never have come into existence." Such great teachers and men of sterling quality and golden utterance as Antigonus of Soko (I, 3), Hillel (I, 12-14; II, 5-8), Jochanan ben Zakkai (II, 9-19), Gamaliel, whose pupil was Paul, the apostle (I, 16), and Judah, the Prince (II, 1), whose sayings grace the pages of *Abot*, were, as Loeb points out, of the Pharisaic school or party. There is naturally a large literature on the Pharisees. Herford's *Pharisaism* deserves careful perusal. See, also, Josephus (ed. Whiston-Margoliouth), *Antiq.*, XIII, 10.6, XVIII, 1, 2-4; Schurer, *History of the Jews*, etc., II, ii, p. 14 *et seq.*; *Jewish Encyclopedia* and literature mentioned there; Geiger, *Judaism and Its History*, p. 102 *et seq.*, and Friedlander, G., *The Jewish Sources of the Sermon on the Mount*, p. 34 *et seq.*
9. There was another, and apparently older, recension of *Pirke Abot* on which is based the *Abot de-Rabbi Natan*, an *hagadic* or homiletical exposition of *Abot*. Two recensions of *Abot de-Rabbi Natan* exist, and have been edited by Schechter. On this work, see Hoffman, *Die erste Mischna*, p. 26 *et seq.*, Mielziner, article *Abot de-Rabbi Natan*, in *Jewish Encyclopedia*, Strack, *Einleitung*, p. 69 et seq., and Pollak, *Rabbi Nathans System*,

been happily styled "a compendium of practical ethics"[10], and, as Mielziner has said, "these Rabbinical sentences, if properly arranged, present an almost complete code of human duties"[11]. The *Abot* is, then, a sort of moral code.

CONTENTS

Even a superficial reading of *Abot* will bring home to one the fact that it is made up of various strata. In fact, it falls naturally into the following strands or divisions:

A. Chapter I, 1-15: Chronologically arranged sayings of the oldest authorities, from the men of the Great Synagogue to Hillel and Shammai.

B. (1) Chapters I, 16-II, 4: Sayings of the men of the school of Hillel to Rabban Gamaliel (about 230 C.E.), the son of Judah ha-Nasi
(2) Chapter II, 5-8: Additional sayings of Hillel.

C. (1) Chapter II, 9-19: The sayings of Jochanan ben Zakkai, the pupil of Hillel, and of his disciples.
(2) Chapter II, 20-21: The sayings of Rabbi Tarfon, a younger contemporary of Jochanan ben Zakkai.

D. Chapter III: the maxims of seventeen *Tannaim* (authorities mentioned in the *Mishnah*) to the time of and including Rabbi Akiba. These are not arranged in strictly chronological order.

E. Chapter IV: The sayings of twenty-five *Tannaim* after the time of Rabbi Akiba, who were contemporaries of Rabbi Meïr and of Rabbi Judah Ha-Nasi. These are not chronologically arranged.

---

etc., *Introduction*, pp. 7-9. An English translation is found in Rodkinson's edition of the *Talmud*, vol. V, p. 1 *et seq.*
10. Taylor, *loc. cit.* Lazarus, *Ethics of Judaism*, II. 113, calls it "a compendium of ethics."
11. *In Jewish Encyclopedia*, art. *Abot*.

F. (1) Chapter V, 1-18: Anonymous sayings forming a series of groups of ten, seven, and four things, dealing with the creation of the world, with miracles, and with the varieties of men and minds.

(2) Chapter V, 19-22: Anonymous sayings touching upon the varieties of motives and contrasting the good and evil dispositions.

(3) Chapter V, 23: Sayings of Judah ben Tema.

(4) Chapter V, 24: The ages of man.

(5) Chapter V, 25, 26: The sayings of Ben Bag Bag and of Ben He He.

G. Chapter VI: The acquisition of the *Torah;* praise of the *Torah.*

LANGUAGE

The language of *Abot* is easy Mishnaic Hebrew, with portions of four verses (I, 13; II, 7; V, 25, and V, 26) in Aramaic, which is closely related to Hebrew. It is worthy of note that these Aramaic portions originated with the school of Hillel[12].

DEVELOPMENT OF ABOT

It is apparent from the literary construction of *Abot*[13] that it has been

---

12. On the language of the *Mishnah*, see Mielziner, *Introduction to the Talmud*, pp. 15-16, and Lauterbach in *Jewish Encyclopedia*, vol II, p. 614. On the use of Aramaic in the *Mishnah*, see Schurer, *History*, I, ii, p. 8 *et seq.*, and Bacher, in *Jewish Encyclopedia*, art. *Aramaic Language Among the Jews*. Several centuries before the common era, Aramaic was the vernacular of the Jews. Hebrew, however, remained in use as the sacred language (לשון הקודש), it being the language of the learned, and was employed for literary, liturgical, and legal purposes. This accounts for the Mishnah being written almost entirely in Hebrew, though Aramaic was spoken on the streets. It is related of Judah ha-Nasi that he disliked the Aramaic jargon to such an extent that he forbade its use in his home, where even the servants spoke Hebrew with elegance (*Rosh ha-Shanah*, 26b). When scholars used Aramaic in his presence, he chided them for not speaking in Hebrew or in Greek (*Baba Kamma*, 82b).

13. *On the subject-matter of this section, consult Hoffmann, Die erste Mischna, pp. 26-37; idem, Mischnaiot Seder Nesikin, Introd., pp. XX-XXI; Brull, Enstehung und ursprunglicher Inhalt des Traktates Abot; Loeb, La Chaine, etc.; Ginzburg, Spruche der Vater, erstes Capitel historisch beleuchtet (Liepzig, 1889); Strack, Die Spruche der Vater, Introd., pp. 7-8; idem, Einleitung, p. 52, and Rawicz, Commentar des Maimonides, p. 105, n. 3.*

edited several times, and that, in its earliest form, the *Abot* collection was much smaller than we have it to-day. Originally, probably shortly after the time of Hillel, it may have been merely a sort of appendix to the *Tractate Sanhedrin*, with typical sayings of each of the heads of the *Sanhedrin*. These dicta are contained in what is designated as section A. Later, presumably by Rabbi Akiba, there were added to this original kernel of *Abot* the sayings of Rabbi Jochanan ben Zakkai and his most illustrious pupils, which comprise section C. This resulted in the grouping together of the sayings of ten generations of traditional authorities, as follows: (1) the men of the Great Synagogue, (2) Simon, the Just, (3) Antigonus of Soko, (4) Jose ben Joezer and Jose ben Jochanan, (5) Joshua ben Perachiah and Nittai, the Arbelite, (6) Judah ben Tabbai and Simeon ben Shatach, (7) Shemaiah and Abtalion, (8) Hillel and Shammai, (9) Jochanan ben Zakkai, and (10) the latter's disciples. By association of idea with this number ten, there were added to this collection numerical sayings of ten, and, then, others of seven and four, found in chapter V, 1-9 and 10-13.

Into this enlarged kernel of pithy sayings of the oldest authorities, which may be characterized as the *Abot of Rabbi Akiba*, later *Tannaim*—Rabbi Meïr, Rabbi Judah ha-Nasi, and others—interpolated additional sayings of the afore-mentioned Rabbis, and also typical utterances of their disciples, and of other well-known teachers. This accounts for the presence in *Abot* of the body of maxims of the six generations of the school of Hillel, designated above as section B 1, and which was very properly introduce after the aphorisms of Hillel and of his contemporary, Shammai. The thread of tradition being interrupted by this interpolation, it was again taken up by the introduction of another body of Hillel's sayings (B 2), thus providing for a natural transition from Hillel to Jochanan ben Zakkai. Proof of the fact that section B is an addition is that in the *Abot de-Rabbi Natan*—which, as has been said above, is based on an older version of *Abot*[14]—the sayings of Jochanan ben Zakkai follow immediately upon those of Shammai. The sayings of Judah ha-Nasi, the

---

14. See *supra*, n. 9.

redactor of the *Mishnah*, and of Rabbi Gamaliel, his son, were undoubtedly added after the time of Judah.

Chapter III contains the sayings of authorities who were the predecessors of Judah, the first two having lived before the destruction of the second Temple. Chapter IV is made up of the dicta of a number of Rabbis who were contemporaries of Judah. These two chapters were, no doubt, inserted by Judah, the redactor of the *Mishnah* as we virtually have it to-day. Evidence that Chapter IV is an addition to the original *Abot* is that it has a number of aphorisms which are repetitions of some found in Chapters I and II. The greater part of Chapter V, as stated above, was a portion of the *Abot* of Rabbi Akiba.

Chapter VI, which is known as *The Chapter on the Acquisition of Torah* (*Perek Kinyan Torah*), as *The External Teaching of the Abot* (*Baraita de-Abot*)[15], as *The Chapter of Rabbi Meïr* (*Perek Rabbi Meïr*)[16], and as *the External Teaching of Rabbi Meïr* (*Baraita de-Rabbi Meïr*), is a supplement of the treatise *Abot*, as is claimed for it by its superscription, "the sages taught in the language of the *Mishnah*," a formula generally used in the *Talmud* to introduce a *Baraita*. One of the authorities mentioned in it is Joshua ben Levi, a Palestinian *amora* (an authority of the *Gemara*) who lived during the third century. This demonstrates the comparatively late date of the final redaction of this chapter. By the middle of the ninth century it formed a part of the treatise *Abot*. It was added to the prayer-book to be read on the sixth Sabbath of the period between Passover and the Festival of Weeks (*Shebuot*)[17].

---

15. A *Baraita* contains traditions and opinions of authorities of the *Mishnah* which are not embodied in the *Mishnah* or Rabbi Judah ha-Nasi. See Mielziner, *Introduction to the Talmud*, pp. 20-21, Strack, *Einleitung in den Talmud*, p. 3, and the *Jewish Encyclopedia*, s.v. A *gemara* (Talmudical commentary) to the *Baraita de-Abot* was published from a MS. by Coronel in *Chamishah Kuntresin* (Vienna, 1864). This *baraita* is found also in the seventeenth chapter of *Tanna de-Be Eliyahu Sutta*, but with different textual readings. See Ginzberg, in the *Jewish Encyclopedia*, II, pp. 516-517.
16. Known thus because Rabbi Meïr's name is found in the first verse.
17. See next section. The sixth chapter is found in some editions of the *Mishnah*.

ABOT IN THE LITURGY

As Taylor has said, "Its simplicity and intrinsic excellence have secured for *Abot*[18] a widespread and lasting popularity, and have led to its being excerpted from the *Talmud* and used liturgically in the Synagogue, at certain seasons, from an early period"[19]. Thus, the *Abot* is found not only in all editions of the *Mishnah* and the *Talmud*, but also in the prayer-books of the Ashkenazic rite[20]. The practice of reading a chapter from *Abot*, on Saturday, after the afternoon prayer (*Minchah*), originated as early as Gaonic times (seventh to eleventh centuries). During the middle of the ninth century, *Abot* and its *Baraita* were thus liturgically used. In Spanish communities it was recited in the morning of the Sabbath, and not in the afternoon. By the eleventh century, this custom was universally a part of the synagogal service.

Originally, *Abot* was probably read only from Passover to *Shebuot*; and, since this period has generally six Sabbaths, and there are only five chapters of *Abot*, the chapter *Kinyan Torah* was appointed to be read on the sixth Sabbath. Later, the period of the year in which *Abot* was read varied in different communities. In Germany, there were *kehillot* in which it was recited during the winter as well as during the summer. In some communities it was read from Passover to the Feast of Tabernacles (*Sukkot*), in others from the Sabbath of *Parashah Yitro* (Ex. XVIII, 1-XX, 26) to the Sabbath of *Parashah Masse'e* (Num. XXXIII, 1-XXXVI, 13), that is, from the Sabbath on which is read an account of the giving of the Law until the Sabbath preceding the beginning of the reading of the "repetition of the Law," *i.e.*, Deuteronomy. In many orthodox congregations to-day this practice

---

18. On the subject-matter of this section, see the citation from the Sar Shalom Gaon, in the *Siddur* of R. Amram, 30a; *Midrash Shemual*, pp. 3-4; Zunz, *Die Ritus*, pp. 85-86; Strack, *Die Spruche der Vater*, p. 5, and *Siddur*, ed. Baer, p. 271, note. Other portions of the *Mishnah* and also of the *Talmud* that are included in the liturgy are, in the morning service, *Zebachim* V (*Siddur*, ed. Singer, p. 11); in the evening service for the Sabbath, *Sabbat*, II (pp. 120-122), and, from the *Talmud*, end of *Berachot* (p. 122); in the additional service for Sabbath and festivals, from the *Talmud Keritot*, 6a, from the *Mishnah*, end of *Tamid*, and from the *Talmud*, end of *Berachot* (pp. 167-168).
19. Taylor, *loc. cit.*
20. German and Polish.

is still adhered to, and *Abot* is read on Sabbath afternoons during the summer, or from the Sabbath after Passover to the Sabbath before the New Year (*Rosh ha-Shanah*).

A number of reasons have been suggested for the custom of reading the *Abot* in the synagogue, the most likely being that it was introduced to occupy the minds of worshippers during the long wait, on a summer's day, between the afternoon and evening services. Whatever the reason for this custom may have been is immaterial and unimportant; but what is of importance is that, by this excellent practice, a whole body of moral dicta—each one summing up with remarkable conciseness a life's experience and philosophy, each one breathing the spirit of piety, saintliness, justice, and love for humanity—has sunk deeply into the innermost heart and consciousness of the Jewish people, exerting such an influence that the principles set forth in the *Abot* have been eternally wrought into the moral fibre of the descendants of the Rabbis. To the lips of the Jew, these maxims spring spontaneously; to those who know them they are a safe and secure guide through life; they are not only heard in the synagogue, but are quoted and applied at home and abroad. Such are the fruits of a benign custom, which Israel will do well to prize and preserve.

BIBLIOGRAPHY

Because of its great popularity, the *Pirke Abot* has appeared in many editions. There is no *Gemara* (Talmudic commentary) on the *Abot*, which undoubtedly accounts for the numerous commentaries on it [21]. Because of the attractiveness of its contents, and since it forms a

---

21. There are more than thirty-five. The best known is that of Maimonides (1135-1204), which was written originally in Arabic, as part of his commentary on the *Mishnah*. A commentary has been attributed to Rashi. Other commentaries are by (1) Rabbi Jacob ben Shimshon, found in the *Machzor Vitry* (see Taylor, *Introd.*, p. 5; *Appendix*, p. 23; (2) Rabbi Israel of Toledo, in Arabic (twelfth to thirteenth century; see Taylor, *Introd.*, p. 5, *Appendix*, p. 46 et seq.; (3) Simon Duran (1361-1444), *Magen Abot;* first edition, Livorno, 1763; ed. Jellinek, Leipzig, 1855; (4) Bertinora (died 1510), in his popular commentary on the *Mishnah;* (5) Isaac ben Judah Abrabanel, *Nachalot Abot;* ed. Constantinople, 1505; (6) Samuel de Uceda, *Midrash Shemual;* venice, 1579, 1585, 1597, 1600, Cracow, 1594, Frankfurt a. M., 1713, Warsaw, 1876; (7) Yom Tob Lippman

part of the ritual, it has been translated many times into many tongues[22], and a great deal has been written on it. The following bibliography will be helpful to the general reader and to the student who wish to get a more detailed and intimate knowledge of the *Abot* than can be imparted in this work.

Editions[23], Commentaries, and Translations

1. Joshua ben Mordecai Falk ha-Kohen, *Abne Yehoshua al Pirke Abot* (New York, 1860). Text and commentary[24].
2. Abraham Geiger, *Pirke Aboth*, in *Nachgelassene Schriften* (Berlin, 1877), vol. IV, pp. 281-344. A commentary on Chaps. I-III. Scholarly and valuable.
3. Solomon Schechter, *Abot de-Rabbi Natan* (Vienna, 1877). Contains two versions, A and B, with an introduction and notes in Hebrew. A scholarly and valuable work.
4. Joseph Jabetz, *Pirke Abot*, with a commentary (Warsaw, 1880).
5. *Charles Taylor, (1) Sayings of the Jewish Fathers, Comprising Pirqe Aboth and Perek R. Meïr in Hebrew and English, with Notes and Excurses. Second edition (Cambridge, 1897). (2) An Appendix of the Sayings of the Jewish Fathers, Containing a Catalogue of Manuscripts and Notes on the Text of Aboth (Cambridge, 1900). These works are very comprehensive and full of valuable material.*

Heller (1579-1654), in *Tosefot Yom Tob*, on the *Mishnah;* (8) elijah, Gaon of Wilna (1720-1797), in *Siddur Tefillat Yacob*, Berlin, 1864; and (9) S. Baer, in *Siddur Abodat Yisroel*, Rodelheim, 1868. There is also acommentary, by Naphtali Herts Wessely, known as *Yayin Lebanon*, Berlin, 1774-1775, which has been translated into English, in the *Hebrew Review* (edited by Morris J. Raphall, London, 1835-1837), Vol. I, p. 177, p. 193, and further.

22. Mischoff, in his *Kritische Geschichte der Talmud-Uebersetzungen aller Zeigen und Zungen* (Frankfurt a. M., 1899), § 56, has a list of 62 translations and of 15 partial translations. Others have appeared since this list was made. For English translation, consult this list.

23. A list of editions, mostly earlier than those mentioned here, and of the *Abot* in *Mishnah* editions may be found in Steinschneider, *Catalogue Librorum Hebraeorum in Bibliotheca Bodleiana* (Berlin, 1852-1860), No. 1433-1519, 1982-2034; M. Roest, *Catalog der Hebraica und Judaica* (Amsterdam, 1875), pp. 818-821, 824-828; and Strack, *Spruche*, pp. 8-9.

24. Falk has been called the "father of American Hebrew literature."

6. A. Berliner, *Commentar zu den Spruchen der Vater, aus Machzor Vitry, mit Beitragen (Frankfurt a. M., 1897).*

7. David Hoffmann, *Masseket Abot*, in *Mischnaiot Seder Nesikin* (Berlin, 1899), pp. 327-367. Fully annotated, with a translation in German, and constant reference to Rabbinical sources. Excellent.

8. Hermann L. Strack, *Die Spruche der Vater*, ein ethischer Mischna-Traktat, third edition (Leipzig, 1901). An excellent text with notes. Very valuable.

9. Lazarus Goldschmidt, in *Talmud Babli, Der Babylonische Talmud* (Berline, 1903), vol. VII, p. 1151 *et seq.* Based on oldest texts of *Abot*. Textual variants and German translation with notes. Very valuable.

10. Simeon Singer, *Perke Abot, Ethics of the Fathers*, in *The Authorized Daily Prayer Book.* Eighth edition (London, 5668-1908), pp. 184-209. Hebrew text, with an excellent English translation, and a few notes.

11. Kaim Pollak, *Rabbi Nathans System der Ethik un Moral* (Budapest, 1905). A translation in German, with notes, of *Abot de Rabbi Natan* (Schechter's version A).

12. Paul Fiebig, *Pirque 'aboth, Der Mischnahtraktat Spruche der Vater* (Tubingen, 1906). German translation and notes, with especial reference to the New Testament. The *Nachwort*, pp. 42-43, consists of a comparison of *Abot* with the New Testament, pointing out the likenesses and differences.

13. Josef ibn Nachmia's, Perush Pirke Abot, *Commentar zu den Pirke Abot . . . nach der Parmaer Hadschrift De Rossi Nr. 1402 . . . mit Anmerkungen von M. L. Bamberger (Berlin, 1907).*

14. M. Rawicz, *Der Commentar der Maimonides zu den Spruchen der Vater, zum ersten Male ins Deutsch ubertragen (Offenberg [Baden], 1910).* Contains "The Eight Chapters"[25].

15. *Sefer Musar, Kommentar zum Mischnatraktat Aboth von R. Joseph*

---

25. The *Eight Chapters* is the introduction of Maimonides to his commentary on *Abot*. Its Hebrew name is *Shemonah Perakim*. It is a remarkable instance of the harmonious welding of the ethical principles contained in *Abot* with mediaeval Aristotelian philosophy.

ben Jehudah. Zum ersten Male herausgegeben von Dr. Wilhelm Bacher. In the Schriften des Vereins Makize Nirdamim. 3. Folge, Nr. 6 (Berlin, 1910).

16. M. Lehmann, *Pirke Aboth, Spruche der Vater uberzetzt und erklart* (Frankfurt a. M., 1909).

17. Jehudah Leb Gordon, *Perki Abot*, in *Siddur Bet Yehudah* (New York, 5672, 1911-12), pp. 106-165. Prayer-book according to the Ashkenazic rite, with Yiddish translation and notes. Contains biographical sketches of all the authorities mentioned in *Abot*.

18. Jules Wolff, *Les Huit Chapitres de Maimonide, ou Introduction à la Mischna d'Aboth, Maximes des Pères (de la Synagogue). Traduits de l'Arabe* (Lausanne, Paris, 1912).

19. Joseph I. Gorfinkle, *The Eight Chapters of Maimonides on Ethics, Edited, Annotated, and Translated with an Introduction* (New York, 1912). Columbia University Oriental Studies, vol. VII[26].

Homiletical Works

1. Lazarus Adler, *Spruche der Vater* (Furth, 1851).
2. W. Aloys Meisel, *Homilien uber die Spruche der Vater* (1885).
3. Alexander Kohut, *The Ethics of the Fathers* (New York, 1885). Translated from the German by Max Cohen.

General Works

Abelson, J. *The Immanence of God in Rabbinical Literature* (London, 1912).

Bacher, Wilhelm, (1) *Die Agada der Tanaiten*, I, II, (Strassburg, 1884, 1890). (2) *Zwei alte Abotkommentare*, in *Monatschrift fur Geschichte und Wiss. d. Judenthums*, 1095, pp. 637-666; 1906, pp. 248-248.

Brull, *Enstehung und ursprunglicher Inhalt des Traktates Abot*, in *Jahrbucher fur Jud. Geschichte und Lit.*, VII (1885).

Danziger, *Jewish Forerunners of Christianity* (New York, 1903).

Dukes, *Rabbinische Blumenlese* (Leipzig, 1844), pp. 67-84.

Friedlander, M. *The Jewish Religion* (London, 1902).

---

[26]. A list of MSS., editions, translations, and commentaries of the *Eight Chapters*, some including *Abot*, is found on pp.27-33 of this work.

Friedlander, G., *The Jewish Sources of the Sermon on the Mount* (London, 1911).

Geiger, *Judaism and its History* (New York, 1911).

Graetz, *History of the Jews*.

Herford, *Pharasaism* (London, 1912).

Hoffmann, *Die erste Mischna und die Contraversen der Tannaim* (Berlin, 1882).

Isaacs, *Stories from the Rabbis* (New York, 1893).

Jewish Encyclopedia.

Josephus, *Antiquities*.

Jung, *Kritik der samtlichen Bucher Aboth in der althebraischen Literatur* (Leipzig, 1888).

Lazarus, *The Ethics of Judaism* (Philadelphia, 1900).

Loeb, (1) *La Chaîne de la Tradition dans le premier Chapitre des Pirke Abot*, in *Bibliothèque de l'école des hautes Études, Sciences religieuses*, vol. I, pp. 307-322 (Paris, 1889). (2) *Notes sur le chapitre Ier des Perke Abot*, in *Revue des Études Juives*, Vol. XIX (1889), pp. 188-201.

Mielziner, (1) *Introduction to the Talmud*, second edition (New York, 1903). (2) Articles *Abot* and *Abot de-R. Natan*, in *Jewish Encyclopedia*.

Myers, *The Story of the Jewish People*, I (New York and London, 1909).

Schechter, *Some Aspects of Rabbinic Theology* (New York, 1909).

Schurer, *Some Aspects of the Jewish People in the Time of Jesus Christ*[27] (New York, 1891), I, i, p. 124; I, ii, p. 353 et seq.; III, ii, p. 30 et seq.

Strack, *Einleitung in den Talmud*, fourth edition (Leipzig, 1908).

Zunz, (1) *Die Gottesdienstlichen Vortrage der Juden* (Berlin, 1832), p. 101 et seq. (2) *Die Ritus des Synagogalen Gottesdienstes* (Berlin, 1859).

---

27. Contains very full bibliographies and has other excellent characteristics, but it is a work that must be used with caution. Its chief fault, according to Schechter, is that it is one of a class of works in which "no attempt is made ... to gain acquaintance with the inner life of the Jewish nation" (*Studies*, II, pp. 119-120).

SAYINGS OF THE FATHERS

One of the following chapters is read on each Sabbath from the Sabbath after Passover until the Sabbath before New Year.

All Israel[1] have a portion in the world to come, and it is said, "And thy people shall be all righteous; they shall inherit the land[2] for ever, the branch of my planting, the work of my hands, that I may be glorified"[3].

---

1. This does not mean that Israel alone, to the exclusion of other nations, will have a portion in the future world. On the future world (העולם הבא), see *the following chap*ter, n. 21. "The pious of all nations have a portion in the world to come" (*Tosefta Sanhedrin*, chap. XII; Maimonides, in *Mishneh Torah*, I, *Hilchot Teshubah*, iii, 5) sums up the Rabbinic opinion.
2. *I.e.*, the land of everlasting life.
3. *Sanhedrin*, X (XI), 1; Isaiah lx, 21. This passage is recited before each chapter.

CHAPTER ONE

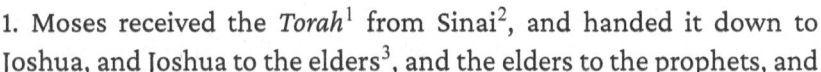

1. Moses received the *Torah*[1] from Sinai[2], and handed it down to Joshua, and Joshua to the elders[3], and the elders to the prophets, and

---

1. The word *Torah* is usually translated by "law," but it means rather "teaching," "instruction" of any kind, or "doctrine." This term is generally used to designate the *Five Books of Moses* or the *Pentateuch*, called the "written law" (תּוֹרָה שֶׁבִּכְתָבה), but it is also employed as a designation of the whole of the Old Testament. Besides the "written law," according to tradition, there was also communicated to Moses, on Mt. Sinai, the "oral law" (תּוֹרָה שֶׁבְּעַל־פֶּה), supplementing the former and other laws and maxims, and explaining it. This "oral law" was handed down by word of mouth from generation to generation, but subsequently, after the destruction of the second Temple, it was committed to writing, and constitutes the *Mishnah*, the *Talmud*, and the *Midrashim*. The "oral law" develops, illuminates, and comments upon the "written law." Here, *Torah* means the "oral law," which Moses communicated to Joshua, Joshua, in turn, to the elders, and so on. See Taylor, *Sayings of the Jewish Fathers*, p. 105 *et seq.*, and 134-135; Friedlander, *The Jewish Religion*, p. 136 *et seq.*; *Jewish Encyclopedia*, arts. *Law and Oral Law*; Schechter, *Some Aspects of Rabbinic Theology*, Chapter VIII; Strack, *Einleitung*, pp. 9-10, and Herford, *Pharisaism*, chapter on "the Theory of Torah," p. 57 *et seq.*
2. *I.e.*, from God. Compare the expression הלכה למשה מסיני, "the law to Moses from Sinai (God)," *Peah*, II, 6, *Eduyot*, VIII, 7, etc.
3. The elders were the wise men who were the members of the supreme national tribunal. See Joshua XXIV, 31.

the prophets delivered it to the men of the Great Synagogue[4]. They said three things, "Be deliberate in judgment; raise up many disciples; and make a fence about the *Torah*"[5].

---

4. The Great Synagogue, whose establishment, after the return from Babylonian captivity, tradition attributes to Ezra the Scribe, consisted of 120 men, who comprised the highest judicial tribunal, and who occupied a position in the early days of the Temple similar to that of the later *Sanhedrin*. The historical foundation of this tradition is Nehemiah VIII-X, in which is recounted the solemn acceptance of the Law by a great assembly of the people. The men of the Great Synagogue appear here in *Abot* as the depositaries of the tradition of the *Torah*, coming in the chain between the last prophets and the earliest scribes. From this chapter and other Rabbinical sources, we gather that the men of the Great Synagogue constituted a sort of college of teachers, one of the last survivors being Simon, the Just (Chapter I, 2). Their work was to interpret, teach, and develop the *Torah*, and to them were ascribed all kinds of legal enactments. They instituted the *Shemoneh Esrah* (the Eighteen Benedictions) and other prayers, and cast the entire ritual into definite shape. They admitted *Proverbs*, the *Song of Songs*, and *Ecclesiastes* into the Old Testament canon. A number of modern scholars, notably Kuenen, are of the opinion that this body never existed in the form represented by Jewish tradition (see Schurer, *History*, I, ii, pp. 354-355). On the controversy regarding the existence of the Great Synagogue see Schechter, *Studies*, II, 105-106. Consult Taylor, *ibid.*, pp. 110-111; Graetz, *History of the Jews*, vol. I, p. 381, 394, vol. II, p. 19. For further bibliography, see Strack, *Spruche*, p. 11. See especially Herford, *Pharisaism*. pp. 18-28.
5. Take measures to prevent the breaking of any of the divine precepts. Thereby, certain things which are in themselves lawful are prohibited in order to enforce the observance of things the doing of which is unlawful. Compare Leviticus XVIII, 30, "make a *mishmeret* to my *mishmeret*" (*Yabamot*, 21a), and *Abot*, III, 17, "the *Massorah* is a fence to the *Torah*."

2. Simon, the Just[6], was of the last survivors of the Great Synagogue. He used to say, "Upon three things the world rests: upon the *Torah*, upon the Temple service[7], and upon the doing of acts of kindness"[8].

3. Antigonus of Soko[9] received (the tradition) from Simon, the Just. He used to say, "Be not like hirelings who work for their master for the sake of receiving recompense; but be like servants who minister to their master without any thought of receiving a reward; and let the fear of Heaven[10] be upon you."

---

6. Simon, the Just, son of Onias, was high-priest about 300 B.C.E. See Josephus, *Antiquities*, XII, ii, 5. Consult Sammter, *Mischnaioth Ordnung Zeraim* (Berlin, 1887), *Introduction*, pp. 10-22; Meilziner, *Introduction to the Talmud*, pp. 22-39; the *Jewish Encyclopedia*, and Strack, *Einleitung*, p. 82 *et seq.*, for the lives of the authorities mentioned in *Abot* and for bibliographies.

7. Cf. *Nedarim*, 32b, "Great is the *Torah*, for if it did not exist, the heaven and the earth would have no permanence." *Abodah* is the service and sacrifice of the Temple which was then standing. After the destruction of the Temple, this word was used to designate the service of prayer. It is used in one of the benedictions after the reading of the *Haftarah*: *al ha-torah we-al ha-abodah*, "for the law and for the divine service," see *Prayer-book*, ed. Singer, p. 149. See Friedlander, *ibid.*, p. 413 *et seq.*

8. גְּמִילוּת חֲסָדִים

"benevolence," "the doing of kindnesses," consists of practical deeds of personal service, as visiting the sick, burying the dead, comforting mourners, peacemaking, etc. It is greater than (tzedakah) "charity" in its narrower sense, as benevolence may be shown to the rich as well as to the poor. See Friedlander, *ibid.*, pp. 301-305. On this verse, see Herford, *ibid.*, p. 22 *et seq.*

9. According to *Abot de-Rabbi Natan*, Chapter V, ed. Schechter, p. 26, Antigonus had two disciples, Zadok and Boethos, from whom arose the Sadducees and the heretical sect of Boethusians, from their misinterpretation of this verse, both denying the doctrines of immortality of the soul and resurrection. Se Kohut, *The Ethics of the Fathers*, p. 43; Schurer, *History*, II, ii. p. 29 *et seq.*; Geiger, *Judaism and Its History*, p. 99 *et seq.*; and *Jewish Encyclopedia*, arts. *Boethusians* and *Sadducees*.

10. "The fear of Heaven" does not mean dread of punishment, but rather awe at the greatness and might of God, and is identical with love and service (see Deuteronomy, VI, 13 and X, 12). It is produced by following out the practices ordained in the *Torah* (Maimonides, *Guide for the Perplexed*, ed. Friedlander, p. 392). Consult Friedlander, *Jewish Religion*, pp. 273-274, the *Jewish Encyclopedia*, art. *Fear of God*, and Schechter, *Aspects*, p. 72.

4. Jose, the son of Joezer, of Zeredah, and Jose, the son of Jochanan[11], of Jerusalem received (the tradition) from them[12]. Jose, the son of Joezer, of Zeredah said, "Let thy house be a meeting-place for the wise; cover thyself with the dust of their feet[13], and drink in their words with thirst."

5. Jose, the son of Jochanan, of Jerusalem said, "Let thy house be open wide; let the poor be members of thy household, and engage not in much gossip with woman." This applies to one's own wife; how much more[14], then, to the wife of one's neighbor? Hence the sages say, "Whoso engages in much gossip with woman brings evil upon himself, neglects the study of the *Torah*, and will in the end inherit *gehinnom*"[15].

6. Joshua, the son of Perachyah, and Nittai, the Arbelite, received (the tradition) from them. Joshua, the son of Perachyah, said, "Provide thyself with a teacher, and possess thyself of a companion[16]; and judge every man in the scale of merit."

---

11. In *Chagigah*, II, 2, we are told that when two leading teachers are named in the *Mishnah* as having received the *Torah*, they constitute a "pair" (זוּג), the first being the president (נָשִׂיא), and the second the vice-president (אָב בֵּית דִּין) of the *Sanhedrin*. There were five pairs of such teachers, flourishing between 170 and 30 B.C.E., the first being Jose b. Joezer and Jose b. Jochanan, and the last being Hillel and Shammai. See Frankel, *Monatschrift*, 1852, pp. 405-421, Mielziner, *Introduction*, pp. 22-23, and Strack, *Spruche*, p. 13.

12. Some texts read "from him" (מִמֶּנּוּ). "From them" must refer to disciples of Antigonus whose sayings have been lost.

13. It was the custom of pupils to sit at the feet of their teachers.

14. On the *kalwa-chomer*, "a conclusion *a minori ad majus*," see Meilziner, *Introduction to the Talmud*, p. 130 *et seq.*, and Strack, *Einleitung in den Talmud*, p. 120. Cf. Chapter VI, 3. The equivalent biblical expression is אפקי.

15. גהינם, גיהנם, גיהינם

    a glen south of Jerusalem where Moloch was worshipped, whence a place where the wicked were punished in the hereafter; "hell, being the opposite of 'the Garden of Eden,'" "paradise." Cf. chapter V, 22 and 23. See Friedlander, *Jewish Religion*, p. 223.

16. A fellow-student.

7. Nittai, the Arbelite, said, "Keep aloof from a bad neighbor[17]; associate not with the wicked, and abandon not the belief in retribution"[18].

8. Judah, the son of Tabbi, and Simeon, the son of Shatach[19], received (the tradition) from them. Judah, the son of Tabbi, said, "(In the judge's office) act not the counsel's part[20]; while the litigants are standing before thee, let them be regarded by thee as guilty, but when they are departed from thy presence, regard them as innocent, the verdict having been acquiesced in by them."

9. Simeon, the son of Shatach, said, "Be very searching in the examination of witnesses[21], and be guarded in thy words, lest through them they learn to lie."

10. Shemaiah and Abtalion[22] received (the tradition) from them. Shemaiah said, "Love work; hate lordship[23]; and seek no intimacy with the ruling power"[24].

---

17. Cf. chapter II, 14.
18. This may mean either that one must not imagine that punishment for evil deeds will not befall him, or when punishment has been meted out, one must not despair of the good.
19. Lived about 104-69 B.C.E. He was a leader of the Pharisees at the time of Alexander Jannaeus.
20. A judge should be strictly impartial.
21. It is related that the son of Simeon b. Shatach was innocently condemned to death, because the witnesses were not carefully cross-questioned.
22. Lived about the middle of the first century B.C.E.
23. "Woe to leadership, for it buries those who possess it." (*Pesachim*, 87b).
24. That is, Rome. Avoid office seeking.

11. Abtalion said, "Ye sages, be heedful of your words, lest ye incur the penalty of exile and be exiled to a place of evil waters, and the disciples who come after you drink thereof and die, and the Heavenly Name be profaned"[25].

12. Hillel and Shammai[26] received (the tradition) from them. Hillel said, "Be of the disciples of Aaron, loving peace and pursuing peace[27], loving mankind and drawing them night to the *Torah*"[28].

13. He used to say, "A name made great is a name destroyed[29]; he who does not increase (his knowledge) decreases (it); and he who does not study deserves to die; and he who makes a worldly use of the crown (of the *Torah*) shall waste away."

---

25. Scholars must be careful in their teachings, lest their disciples misinterpret their words, and thus adopt false doctrines, as was the case with the disciples of Antigonus of Soko (*Supra*, n. 12). "Evil waters" may stand for evil doctrines or evil people. When a teacher went into banishment, he was usually followed by his disciples. Departure from the law is equivalent to death.

26. Hillel and Shammai, the most renowned of the "pairs" (זוגות), lived about 100 years before the destruction of the Temple. Each was the founder of a school, *Bet Hillel* and *Bet Shammai*, being generally opposed to one another in the interpretation of the *Torah*. Hillel was the embodiment of humility, gentleness, and kindness; Shammai was irritable, and lacked gentleness and patience. The former's most celebrated saying is, "What is hateful to thee do not do unto thy fellow man; this is the whole *Torah*, the rest is mere commentary." See Bacher, *Agada der Tanaiten*; Schurer, *History*, I, ii, p. 359 *et seq.*; Myers, *story of the Jewish People*, I, p. 136 *et seq.*; geiger, *Judaism and its History*, p. 113 *et seq.*

27. Psalm XXIV, 15: "Seek peace and pursue it."

28. Draw men to the *Torah* by good example, not by endeavoring to make converts.

29. He who seeks a name loses fame.

14. He used to say, "If I am not for myself, who will be for me? But if I care for myself only, what am I?[30]. And if not now, when?"

15. Shammai said, "Set a fixed time for thy (study of) *Torah;* say little and do much[31]; and receive all men with a cheerful countenance."

16. Rabban[32] Gamaliel said, "Provide thyself with a teacher; be quit of doubt[33]; and accustom not thyself to give tithes[34] by a conjectural estimate."

17. Simeon[35] his son, said, "All my days I have grown up amongst the wise, and I have found nothing better for man than silence[36]; not learning but doing is the chief thing[37]; and whoso multiplies words causes sin"[38].

---

30. Be self-reliant, but not selfish.
31. Or "promise little." Be like Abraham, who promised only bread, but brought a "calf tender and good" (Genesis XVIII, 5 and 7).
32. "Our teacher," "our master," a title given only to the presidents of the *Sanhendrin*, Gamaliel being the first to be thus known. Gamaliel was a grandson of Hillel and a teacher of Paul. See Strack, *Einleitung*, p. 85.
33. Establish over you the authority of a teacher, to hold you from the clutch of doubt (Kohut).
34. There were three kinds of tithes (the tenth part of anything): (a) "the first tithe" (*maaser rishon*), given to the Lebites; "the second tithe" (*maaser sheni*), taken to Jerusalem and consumed there by the owner and his family; and (c) the tithe paid to the poor (*maaser ani*). See Leviticus XXVII, 30 *et seq.*, Numbers XVIII, 21-24, and Deuteronomy XIV, 22-29; also *Tractates Maasrot* and *Maaser Sheni* of the *Mishnah*. Consult Babbs, *The Law of Tithes*.
35. Simeon beg Gamaliel I lived at the time of the war with Rome. See Josephus, *Jewish Wars*, IV, 3, 9.
36. Cf. chapter III, 17.
37. Where words fail, deeds tell. *Non scholae sed vitae.*
38. Cf. Proverbs X, 19.

18. Rabban Simeon, the son of Gamaliel[39] said, "By three things is the world preserved[40]; by truth, by judgment, and by peace, as it is said, 'Judge ye the truth and the judgment of peace in your gates'"[41].

Rabbi Chanania[42], the son of Akashia, said, "The Holy One, blessed be He, was pleased to make Israel worthy; wherefore He gave them a copious *Torah* and many commandments, as it is said, 'It pleased the Lord, for his righteousness' sake, to magnify the *Torah* and make it honorable'"[43].

---

39. Rabban Simeon II, son of Gamaliel II (80-115 C.E.) and grandson of Simeon (verse 17).
40. Cf. chapter I, 2. *Torah*, Temple service, and benevolence are the foundations and, at the same time, the aims of the world. Truth, judgment, and peace maintain the world's permanency.
41. Zechariah VIII, 16.
42. This saying did not belong originally to *Abot*, but was taken from *Makkot*, III, 16. According to Goldschmidt, it was introduced into the *Mishnah* from the separate editions, and then found its way into the Talmudical texts of *Abot*. This verse is recited at the end of each chapter. See Rawicz, *Commentor des Maimonides*, p. 114, n. 1.
43. Isaiah, xlii, 21.

CHAPTER TWO

All Israel[1,2] have a portion in the world to come, and it is said, "And thy people shall be all righteous; they shall inherit the land[3] for ever, the branch of my planting, the work of my hands, that I may be glorified"[4].

1. Rabbi[5] said, "which is the right course that a man should choose

---

1. The original text included the phrase "All Israel," etc., on page 29, as the opening line of the chapter, with the page numbers indicating the start of Chapter I. Instead of referencing these sentences in the same way, this version places them directly in their intended positions within the text. The editor believes this method better captures the essence of the original material.
2. This does not mean that Israel alone, to the exclusion of other nations, will have a portion in the future world. On the future world (העולם הבא), see *the following chap*ter, n. 21. "The pious of all nations have a portion in the world to come" (*Tosefta Sanhedrin*, chap. XII; Maimonides, in *Mishneh Torah*, I, *Hilchot Teshubah*, iii, 5) sums up the Rabbinic opinion.
3. *I.e.*, the land of everlasting life.
4. *Sanhedrin*, X (XI), 1; Isaiah lx, 21. This passage is recited before each chapter.
5. Rabbi Judah (135-220 C.E.), son of Simeon (chapter I, 18), was known as "Rabbi," as a mark of distinction, owing to the fact that he was the chief reviser and compiler of the *Mishnah*. Earlier compilers of the *Mishnah* had been Hillel, Akiba, and R. Meïr.

for himself?[6] That which is a pride to him who pursues it and which also brings him honor from mankind. Be as scrupulous about a light precept as about a grave one, for thou knowest not the grant of reward for each precept. Reckon the loss incurred by the fulfilment of a precept against the reward secured by its observance[7], and the gain gotten by a transgression against the loss it involves. Consider three things, that thou mayest not come within the power of sin[8]. Know what is above thee—a seeing eye, and a hearing ear, and all thy deeds written in a book"[9].

2. Rabban Gamaliel, the son of Rabbi Judah, the Prince, said, "Excellent is the study of *Torah* combined with some worldly pursuit[10], for the effort demanded by them both makes sin to be forgotten. All study of *Torah* without work must at length be futile,

---

Rabbi Judah was also known as *Rabbenu* (our Master), *ha-Nasi* (the Prince), and *ha-Kodesh* (the Holy). He is said to have died on the day that Akiba met his death at the hands of the Romans. See Danziger, *Jewish Forerunners of Christianity*, pp. 242-274, Myers, *Story of the Jewish People*, I, 210-222, and Strack, *Einleitung in den Talmud*, p. 96.
6. Maimonides interprets this verse as meaning to pursue a medium course between two equally bad extremes, the *too much* and the *too little*. On this subject, see his celebrated fourth chapter of the *Shemonah Perakim* (*The Eight Chapters*) on the "mean"; ed. Gorfinkle, p. 54, *et seq*.
7. I.e., the loss in this world as against the reward in the future world. On the Rabbinic idea of reward and punishment, see Schechter, *Aspects*, pp. 162-163, and Herford, *Pharisaism*, p. 267 *et seq*.
8. Cf. chapter III, 1. No deeds, great or small, are lost sight of by God.
9. On the divine books or book, see Exodus XXXII, 35. Malachi III, 16, and Daniel VII, 10, etc. The heavenly "Book of Life" is prominently mentioned in the ritual of the New Year and the Day of Atonement, especially in the celebrated prayer, *U-netanneh Tokef* of Rabbi Amnon of Mayence. The New Year's greeting, "May you be inscribed for a happy year!" is evidence of the popularity of the idea of a divine book in which the fate of a man is written. See the *Jewish Encyclopedia*, art. *Book of Life*.
10. The expression *Talmud Torah* (lit., "study of the Law") means the study of all sacred learning. The word *Torah*, here, is to be construed in its broadest sense. See chapter I, n. 4. Such study was one of the duties to which no limit was fixed (*Peah* I, 1). The expression ארץ דרך means "good manners" (chapter III, 21), or "worldly business," or "care" (chapter III, 6), according to the context. Study combined with some trade or profession is, according to R. Gamaliel, the proper thing. See chapter IV, n. 24.

and leads to sin[11]. Let all who are employed with the congregation act with them for Heaven's sake, for then the merit of their fathers sustains them, and their righteousness endures for ever[12]. And as for you (God will then say), 'I account you worthy of great reward, as if you had wrought it all yourselves.'

3. Be on your guard against the ruling power[13]; for they who exercise it draw no man near to them except for their own interests; appearing as friends when it is to their own advantage, they stand not by a man in the hour of his need."

4. He used to say, "Do His will as if it were thy will. Nullify thy will before His will, that He may nullify the will of others before thy will."

5. Hillel[14] said, "Separate not thyself from the congregation[15]; trust not in thyself until the day of thy death[16]; judge not thy neighbor until thou art come into his place; and say not anything which cannot be understood at once, in the hope that it will be understood

---

11. Cf. *Kiddushin*, 29a, "He who does not teach his son a trade teaches him to be a thief."
12. In every community, the work and goodness of past generations live in the present, and the good that the community does in the present will live on in the future. On the "merit of the fathers (זכו׳ת אבות), see Schechter, *Some Aspects of Rabbinic Theology*, chapter XII, especially pp. 175-177, where this passage is quoted.
13. This verse is directed toward the leaders of the community. Cf. above, chapter I, 10.
14. The chain of traditional sayings is continued here from chapter I, 14, with other maxims of Hillel. See *Introduction*.
15. I.e., share its weal and woe. Cf. *Taanit*, 11a, "He who does not join the community in times of danger and trouble will never enjoy the divine blessing."
16. One should constantly be on guard against oneself. The *Talmud* (*Berachot*, 29a) illustrates this saying by referring to a certain Jochanan, who, after having been high-priest for eighty years, became a heretic.

in the end[17]; neither say, 'When I have leisure I will study'; perchance thou wilt have no leisure."

6. He used to say, "An empty-headed man cannot be a sin-fearing man, nor can an ignorant person[18] be pious, nor can a shamefaced man[19] learn, nor a passionate man[20] teach, nor can one who is engaged overmuch in business grow wise[21]. In a place where there are no men, strive to be a man"[22].

7. Moreover, he once saw a skull floating on the surface of the water. He said to it, "Because thou didst drown (others) they have drowned thee, and at the last they that drowned thee shall themselves be drowned"[23].

---

17. This verse may be variously translated and interpreted. Its translation here is in accordance with the interpretation of Maimonides. Do not express yourself in such a way that your words may be understood only after careful study and deep thought, but let them be clear and intelligible.
18. The word בור means "uncultivated" שדה בור "an uncultivated field". It is used of an ignorant, uncultured, mannerless person, possessing no moral or spiritual virtues. Taylor translates it by "boor." אני הארץ, literally "people of the land," "country people," is applied to an individual who may possess good manners, and may be literate, but who has no religious knowledge, nor training, nor does not observe religious customs. Taylor renders it "vulgar." Mayer Sulzberger maintains that this term was applied to an assembly of representatives of the people constituting a body similar to the modern Parliament, and divided into a lower and upper house. See his "*The Am Ha-aretz, The Ancient Hebrew Parliament.*" On the *Am ha-aretz* and his opposite the *chaber*, see Schurer, *History*, II, ii, pp. 8, 9 and pp. 22 *et seq.*, also Herford, *ibid.* pp. 46-47.
19. *I.e.*, he who is ashamed to ask questions for fear of exposing his ignorance.
20. He who has no patience to answer all the questions of his pupils.
21. Cf. chapter IV, 12. One of the qualifications necessary for the acquirement of the *Torah* is moderation in business.
22. Do not boldly push yourself forward; but where there is no one to fill the position of teacher or leader, or to be the head of the community, and you have the qualifications, do not shrink from being the man.
23. Retribution is sure. Cf. *Sanhedrin*, 100a and *Sotah*, 9b, "with what measure a man measures, is it measured unto him."

8. He used to say, "The more flesh, the more works; the more property, the more anxiety; the more women, the more witchcraft; the more maid-servants, the more lewdness; the more men-servants, the more robbery; the more *Torah*, the more life[24]; the more schooling, the more wisdom; the more counsel, the more understanding; the more charity, the more peace. He who has acquired a good name has acquired it for himself; he who has acquired for himself words of *Torah* has acquired for himself life in the world to come"[25].

9. Rabban Jochanan, the son of Zakkai[26] received (the tradition) from Hillel and Shammai. He used to say, "If thou hast learnt much *Torah*, ascribe not any merit to thyself, for thereunto wast thou created."

10. Rabban Jochanan, the son of Zakkai, had five disciples[27], and these are they: Rabbi Eliezer, the son of Hyrcanus; Rabbi Joshua, the

---

24. Cf. Prov. III, 1 and 2.
25. The expression "the world to come" may mean the Messianic days, the time after the Messianic era, the days after the resurrection or the spiritual hereafter. Maimonides discusses at length the various theories, in *Perek Chelek* (Commentary on *Sanhedrin*, X, 1), which has been translated into English by J. Abelson, in the *Jewish Quarterly Review* (London), vol. XXIX, p. 28 *et seq.* See also *The Hebrew Review* (London, 1840), p. 254 *et seq.* Consult Schurer, *History*, II, ii, 92.
26. Rabban Jochanan ben Zakkai was known as the least of the disciples of Hillel. He was a contemporary of the historian Josephus. Escaping in a coffin from Jerusalem, when it was besieged by the Roman general Vespasian, and predicting the latter's elevation to the imperial dignity, Jochanan was allowed by Vespasian to go to Jabneh (Jamnia), where he founded the celebrated academy which became the centre of learning in Palestine, as Jerusalem had previously been. He was the most important scribe in the first decade after the destruction of the Temple (70 C.E.). See Strack, *Einleitung in den Talmud*, p. 86 *et seq.*, Bacher, *Agada der Tanaiten*, pp. 25-46, Myers, *Story of the Jewish People*, I, pp. 151-160, and Danziger, *Jewish Forerunners of Christianity*, pp. 55-72.
27. Of special excellence.

son of Hananiah[28]; Rabbi Jose, the Priest; Rabbi Simeon, the son of Nataniel; and Rabbi Eleazar, the son of Arach.

11. He used thus to recount their praise: "Eliezer, the son of Hyrcanus, is a cemented cistern, which loses not a drop[29]; Joshua, the son of Hananiah, happy is she that bare him[30]; Jose, the Priest, is a pious man[31]; Simeon, the son of Nataniel, is a fearer of sin; Eleazar, the son of Arach, is like a spring flowing with ever-sustained vigor"[32].

12. He used to say, "If all the sages of Israel were in one scale of the balance, and Eliezer, the son of Hyrcanus, in the other, he would outweigh them all." Abba Saul[33] said in his name, "If all the sages of Israel were in one scale of the balance, and Eliezer, the son of Hyrcanus, also with them, and Eleazar, the son of Arach, in the other scale, he would outweigh them all."

13. He said to them, "Go forth and see which is the good way to which a man should cleave." R. Eliezer said, "A good eye"[34]; R. Joshua said, "A good friend"; R. Jose said, "A good neighbor"[35]; R. Simeon

---

28. On the life of R. Joshua (40-130 C.E.), see Bacher, *ibid.*, 129-194, Myers, *ibid.*, 161-170, Danziger, *ibid.*, 122-151.
29. He forgets nothing he has learned. On R. Eliezer, see Danziger, *ibid.*, 91-121.
30. When yet a child in the cradle, his mother took him into the synagogue that he might thus early hear the words of the *Torah*.
31. A *chasid* (חסיד), "saint," is one who does more than the strict letter of the law requires. See Schechter, *Studies*, II, pp. 148-181, *idem*, *Aspects*, p. 209, Rawicz, *Commentar des Maimonides*, pp. 95-96, and Gorfinkle, *The Eight Chapters*, pp. 60-62.
32. "A welling spring" (Taylor).
33. He lived in the first half of the second century, C.E.
34. *I.e.*, an eye that looks upon people with benevolence and kind feelings, free from envy and ill-will.
35. A good friend is one who induces his associate to study *Torah*, and who reproves

said, "One who foresees the fruit of an action"[36]; R. Eleazar said, "A good heart." Thereupon he said to them, "I approve of the words of Eleazar, the son of Arach, rather than your words, for in his words yours are included"[37].

14. He said to them, "Go forth and see which is the evil way that a man should shun." R. Eliezer said, "An evil eye"[38]; R. Joshua said, "A bad friend"; R. Jose said, "A bad neighbor"; R. Simeon said, "One who borrows and does not repay—it is the same whether one borrows from man or the Omnipresent[39]; as it is said, 'The wicked borroweth and payeth not again, but the righteous dealeth graciously and giveth'"[40]; R. Eleazar said, "A bad heart." Thereupon he said to them, "I approve of the words of Eleazar, the son of Arach, rather then your words, for in his words yours are included."

15. They each said three things. R. Eliezer said, "Let thy friend's honor be as dear to thee as thine own[41]; be not easily excited to anger; and repent one day before thy death"[42]. And (he further said),

---

36. One who balances the present against the future.
37. The heart was considered the seat of all moral and spiritual functions. See Schechter, *Aspects*, p. 255 *et seq.*
38. Denotes niggardliness, envy, or jealousy.
39. *I.e.*, one who lacks foresight and incurs responsibilities he is unable to meet borrows from God, as all wealth belongs to Him, and men are merely His stewards. The word מקום, literally "place," "space," was used to designate Jerusalem, or the Temple, as being *the* place where God's spirit dwells; or it may also refer to the divine court of the *Sanhedrin*. It then came to be used as an appellative for God. As Schechter remarks, "The term is mainly indicative of God's ubiquity in the world and can best be translated by 'Omnipresent.'" See Hoffmann, *Sanhedrin* VI, note 56, Taylor, *Sayings*, p. 53, note 42, and Schechter, *Aspects*, pp. 26-27, where the literature on this subject is given. See also Friedlander, *The Jewish Religion*, p. 287, and the Jewish Encyclopedia, art. *Names of God.*
40. Psalm XXXVII, 21.
41. Cf. chapter IV, 15.
42. Man should repent every day of his life, for he knows not on what day he may die (*Shabbat*, 153a).

"Warm thyself by the fire of the wise, but beware of their glowing coals, lest thou be burnt, for their bite is the bite of the fox, and their sting is the scorpion's sting, and their hiss is the serpent's hiss, and all their words are like coals of fire"[43].

16. R. Joshua said, "The evil eye, the evil inclination[44], and hatred of his fellow-creatures[45], put a man out of the world."

17. R. Jose said, "Let the property of thy friend be as dear to thee as thine own; prepare thyself for the study of *Torah*, since the knowledge of it is not an inheritance of thine, and let all thy deeds be done in the name of God"[46].

18. R. Simeon said, "Be careful in reading the *Shema*[47] and the

---

43. One who wishes to warm himself remains a certain distance away from the fire; if he approaches too near, he is burned; so, do not endeavor to become too intimate with the wise, as their opinion of you may change to your detriment. The "bite," the "sting," and the "hiss" represent the terribleness of the looks of the wise who have been angered.
44. Passion, evil nature, or evil inclination.
45. Misanthropy.
46. In making man's highest ideal the comprehension of God, Maimonides, in the *Shemonah Perakim*, supports his view by referring to the latter part of this verse. He says, "The sages of blessed memory, too, have summed up this idea in so few words and so concisely, at the same time elucidating the whole matter with such complete thoroughness, that when one considers the brevity with which they express this great and mighty thought in its entirety, about which others have written whole books and yet without adequately explaining it, one truly recognizes that the Rabbis undoubtedly spoke through divine inspiration. This saying is found among their precepts, and is, 'Let all thy deeds be done in the name of God.'" See Gorfinkle, *The Eight Chapters*, p. 73.
47. This prayer consists of three portions of the Pentateuch (Deut. VI, 4-9; XI, 13-21; Num. XV, 37-41), and gets its name from the initial word of the first portion. It is appointed to be read twice daily, in the morning and in the evening. On the time when the *Shema* is to be read, see *Berachot* I, 1. See Schurer, *History*, II, ii, 77, 83, *et seq.*; Fried-

Amidah[48]; and when thou prayest, consider not thy prayer as a fixed (mechanical) task, but as (an appeal for) mercy and grace before the All-present, as it is said, 'For he is gracious and full of mercy, slow to anger, and abounding in loving-kindness, and repenteth him of the evil'[49]; and be not wicked in thine own esteem"[50].

19. R. Eleazar said, "Be diligent in studying *Torah*, and know what answer to give to the unbeliever[51]; know also before whom thou

---

lander, *Jewish Religion*, pp. 430, 435; *Jewish Encyclopedia*, art. *Shema*, and Adler, in the *Jewish Review* (London, 1910), vol. I, number 2, p. 159.

48. An important part of the ritual said at the daily morning, afternoon, and evening service, and also at the additional service on Sabbaths and holy days, is known as (1) *Tefillah* (prayer), or (2) *Shemoneh Esreh* (eighteen), or (3) *Amidah* (standing). It is known as *Tefillah* because it is considered the prayer *par excellence;* as *Shemoneh Esreh* because originally it consisted of eighteen prayers (now nineteen); and as *Amidah* (by Sephardic Jews) because it must be said standing. The *Shema* and the *Shemoneh Esreh* have been appropriately styled the "two pillars of the fabric of the liturgy." See Schurer, *ibid.*; Friedlander, *ibid.*, pp. 430, 437; in the Jewish Encyclopedia, art. *Shemoneh Esreh*; Schechter, *Studies*, II, pp. 67068; Adler, *ibid.*, p. 159; and Herford, *ibid.*, pp. 298-299.

49. Joel II, 13.

50. Do not do what your conscience tells you is wrong, even though it does not appear to others as such; or, do not sin in secret, thinking that you will escape punishment because others do not see you.

51. *Apikuros* is a term originally used to designate a follower of the philosopher Epicurus, whose axiom was that "happiness or enjoyment is the *summum bonum* of life." Later, this word was used by the Rabbis to designate a free-thinker, a heretic, an unbeliever, or a despiser of the Law, Jewish or non-Jewish. Josephus (*Antiquities*, X, 11, 7, ed. Whiston-Margoliouth, p. 300) describes the Epicureans as those "who cast providence out of human life, and do not believe that God takes care of the affairs of the world, nor that the universe is governed and continued in being by that blessed and immortal nature, but say that the world is carried along of its own accord without a ruler and a curator." Maimonides, in his commentary on *Sanhedrin*, X, 1, derives the word from the Hebrew, חופש, "freedom," and defines it as one who refuses obedience to the Law. Schechter (*Studies in Judaism*, I, p. 158) says, "It implies rather a frivolous treatment of the words of Scripture and tradition." See the *Jewish Encyclopedia* art. *Apikuros*, and Barton, *Ecclesiastes*, p. 41. This verse may also be rendered, "Study *Torah*, and also know (ודע) how to answer an unbeliever," meaning that first one should study *Torah* and *Talmud*, and then give his time to learning other knowledge, so as to be able to refute those who stray from the truth.

toilest, and who thy Employer is, who will pay thee the reward of thy labor."

20. Rabbi Tafron[52] said, "The day is short, the task is great[53], the laborers are sluggish, the reward is much, and the Master of the house[54] is urgent."

21. He also used to say, "It is not thy duty to complete the work, but neither art thou free to desist from it; if thou hast studied much *Torah*, much reward will be given thee; and faithful is thy Employer to pay thee the reward of thy labor; and know that the grant of reward unto the righteous will be in the time to come"[55].

Rabbi Chanania, the son of Akashia, said, "The Holy One, blessed be He, was pleased to make Israel worthy; wherefore He gave them a copious *Torah* and many commandments, as it is said, 'It pleased the Lord, for his righteousness' sake, to magnify the *Torah* and make it honorable'".

---

52. A contemporary of Jochanan ben Zakkai's five disciples and of Akiba. See Bacher, *ibid.*, pp. 348-358, and Meyer, *ibid.*, p. 179.
53. The day, *i.e.*, the life of man, is brief. Art is long, but life is short.
54. *I.e.*, God.
55. A man cannot finish the work of the world, yet he must not yield to idleness and despair, but must do his share to the best of his ability. His reward will come in the future.

CHAPTER THREE

All Israel have a portion in the world to come, and it is said, "And thy people shall be all righteous; they shall inherit the land for ever, the branch of my planting, the work of my hands, that I may be glorified".

1. Akabia[1], the son of Mahalalel, said, "Consider three things, and thou wilt not come within the power of sin[2]: know whence thou camest, and whither thou art going, and before whom thou wilt in the future have to give an account and reckoning[3]. Whence thou camest: from a fetid drop; whether thou art going: to a place of dust, worms, and maggots[4]; and before whom thou wilt in the future have

---

1. He lived about the middle of the first century.
2. Cf. chapter II, 1.
3. Compare with this saying the exposition by Akiba of Eccl. XII, 1. If man thinks of whence he comes, he is rendered humble; if he reflects upon whither he is going, he prizes worldly things lightly; and if he considers Him before whom he must give an account, he obeys God's laws.
4. Cf. Job XXV, 6: "How much less the mortal, the mere worm (רימה)? and the son of the earth, the mere maggot (תולעה)?" can be pure in God's eyes.

to give an account and reckoning: before the Supreme King of kings, the Holy One, blessed be He."

2. R. Chanina, the Vice-High-Priest[5], said, "Pray for the welfare of the government, since but for the fear thereof men would swallow each other alive"[6].

3. R. Chananiah, the son of Teradion[7], said, "If two sit together and interchange no words of *Torah*, they are a meeting of scorners, concerning whom it is said, 'The godly man sitteth not in the seat of the scorners'[8]; but if two sit together and interchange words of *Torah*, the Divine Presence[9] abides among them; as it is said, 'Then they that feared the Lord spake one with the other; and the Lord hearkened and heard, and a book of remembrance was written before Him, for them that feared the Lord, and that thought upon His name,'[10]. Now the Scripture enables me to draw this inference in respect to two persons; whence can it be deduced that if even one

---

5. Chief of the priests, adjutant high-priest. The *segan* was next in rank to the high-priest. None could be appointed high-priest unless he had occupied the office of the *segan* (Palestinian *Talmud, Yoma*, III, 41a, top). According to Schurer, he was "the captain of the Temple," whose duty it was to superintend arrangements for keeping order in and around the Temple. He was also present at all important functions in which the high-priest took part, such as the drawing of lots in the case of the two goats on *Yom Kippur* (Yoma III, 9, IV, 1); when reading from the *Torah* (*Yoma*, VII, 1; *Sotah* VII, 7, 8), and when offering the daily sacrifice (*Tamid* VII, 3). Rabbi Chanina was the last to bear this title, his son being known as Simeon ben ha-Segan. See Bacher, *Agada der Tanaiten*, pp. 55-58, Schurer, *History*, II, i, 257-259.

6. Cf. Jer. XXXIX, 7, "And seek the peace of the city whither I have caused you to be carried away captives, and pray unto the Lord for it; for in the peace thereof shall ye have peace," and *Abodah Zarah*, 3b.

7. He lived about 120 C.E. He was the father of Beruriah, the wife of Rabbi Meïr.

8. Ps. I, 1. Verse 2 of this psalm continues, "But his delight is in the Law of the Lord."

9. שכינה

literally "dwelling," is a name applied to God when He is spoken of as dwelling among men. See Schechter, *Aspects, en passim*; Abelson, *Immanence of God*, p. 77 et seq.

10. Mal. III, 16.

person sedulously occupies himself with the *Torah*, the Holy One, blessed be He, appoints unto him a reward? Because it is said, 'though he sit alone, and meditate in stillness, yet he taketh it (the reward) upon him'"[11].

4. R. Simeon[12] said, "If three have eaten at a table and have spoken there no words of *Torah*, it is as if they had eaten of sacrifices to dead idols, of whom it is said, 'For all their tables are full of vomit and filthiness; the All-present is not (in their thoughts)'[13]. But if three have eaten at a table and have spoken there words of *Torah*, it is as if they had eaten at the table of the All-present, for Scripture says, 'And he said unto me, This is the table that is before the Lord'"[14].

5. R. Chanina, the son of Hakinai[15], said, "He who keeps awake at night, and goes on his way alone, while turning his heart to vanity, such a one forfeits his own life"[16].

6. R. Nechunya, son of ha-Kanah[17], said, "Whoso receives upon

---

11. Lam. III, 27.
12. Rabbi Simeon ben Yochai lived about the middle of the second century C.E., and was a pupil of Akiba. See Danziger, *ibid.*, pp. 211-241. He was long thought to be the author of the well-known kabbalistic work *Zohar*, which was, however, probably written in the thirteenth century by Moses Shem Tob de Leon. See the *Jewish Encyclopedia*, art. *Zohar;* Graetz, *History*, IV, p. 11 *et seq.;* Schechter, *Studies*, I, pp. 18, 19, 133; and H. Sperling, in *Aspects of the Hebrew Genius*, p. 165 *et seq.*
13. Isa. XXVIII, 8. The literal interpretation of בלי מקום is, there is "no place" clean of defilement; but the word מקום being used to designate God (see above, chapter II, n. 35), suggests the interpretation, "without mention of the name of God."
14. Ezek. XLI, 22.
15. He lived about 120 C.E., and was a pupil of Akiba. See Bacher, *ibid.*, 436 *et seq.*
16. Even the sleepless man and the solitary traveller must turn their thoughts to the *Torah*.
17. He lived about 80 C.E. See Bacher, *ibid.*, pp. 58-61.

himself the yoke of the *Torah*, from the yoke of the kingdom and the yoke of worldly care will be removed[18], but whoso breaks off from him the yoke of the *Torah*, upon him will be laid the yoke of the kingdom and the yoke of worldly care."

7. R. Chalafta, the son of Dosa[19], of the village of Chanania said, "When ten people sit together and occupy themselves with the *Torah*, the *Shechinah*[20] abides among them, as it is said, 'God standeth in the congregation[21] of the godly'[22]. And whence can it be shown that the same applies to five? Because it is said, 'He hath found his band[23] upon the earth'[24]. And whence can it be shown that the same applies to three? Because it is said, 'He judgeth among the judges'[25]. And whence can it be shown that the same applies to two? Because it is said, 'Then they that feared the Lord spake one with the other; and the Lord hearkened, and heard'[26]. And whence can it be shown that the same applies even to one? Because it is said, 'In every place where I cause my name to be remembered I will come unto thee and I will bless thee'"[27].

---

18. The "yoke of the kingdom" refers to the taxes and burdens exacted by the government; the "yoke of worldly care" is anxiety of the struggle for existence.
19. He was probably a disciple of R. Meïr. See below, n. 32.
20. See above, n. 9.
21. An *edah*, "assembly," "congregation," "prayer-meeting," consists of at least ten persons (*Megillah*, 23b). See Sulzburger, *The Ancient Hebrew Parliament*, chapter I.
22. Ps. LXXXII, 1.
23. An *agudah* (lit., "bundle," "bunch"), "bond," "union," is constituted of at least five, though some authorities maintain that it stands for three. See Taylor, *Sayings*, p. 46, n. 15. This word is used in the name of a number of Jewish societies whose members bind themselves to brotherly love and mutual assistance. as *Agudat Achim*, "United Brethren," etc.
24. Amos, IX, 6.
25. Ps. LXXXII, 1. Every *bet din*, "judicial tribunal," consisted of at least three members (*Sanhedrin*, 3b).
26. Mal. III, 16.
27. Ex. XX, 24.

8. R. Eleazar of Bertota[28] said, "Give unto Him of what is His, for thou and thine are His: this is also found expressed by David, who said, 'For all things come of Thee, and of Thine own we have given Thee'"[29].

9. R. Jacob said, "He who is walking by the way and studying, and breaks off his study and says, 'How fine is that tree, how fine is that fallow,' him the Scripture regards as if he had forfeited his life"[30].

10. R. Dostai[31], the son of Jannai, said in the name of R. Meïr[32], "Whoso forgets one word of his study, him the Scripture regards as if he had forfeited his life, for it is said, 'Only take heed to thyself, and keep thy soul diligently, lest thou forget the things which thine eyes have seen'[33]. Now, one might suppose (that the same result follows) even if a man's study has been too hard for him. (To guard against such an inference), it is said, 'And lest they depart from thy heart all the days of thy life'[34]. Thus a person's guilt is not established until he deliberately and of set purpose removes those lessons from his heart."

---

28. He lived during the second century C.E. See Bacher, *ibid.*, pp. 442-445.
29. I Chron. XXIX, 14.
30. One must not interrupt his studies even to admire the beauties of nature.
31. He lived about 160 C.E.
32. Rabbi Meïr was the celebrated pupil of Akiba. His wife was the well-known Bruriah. On his interesting career, see Blumenthal, *Rabbi Meïr*, Myers, *The Story of the Jewish People*, I, pp. 189-204, and Danziger, *Jewish Forerunners of Christianity*, pp. 185-210.
33. Deut. IV, 9.
34. Deut. IV, 9.

11. R. Chanina, the son of Dosa[35], said, "He in whom the fear of sin precedes wisdom, his wisdom shall endure; but he in whom wisdom comes before the fear of sin, his wisdom will not endure"[36].

12. He used to say, "He whose works exceed his wisdom, his wisdom shall endure; but he whose wisdom exceeds his works, his wisdom will not endure"[37].

13. He used to say, "He in whom the spirit of his fellow-creatures takes not delight, in him the Spirit of the All-present takes not delight."

14. R. Dosa, the son of Horkinas[38], said, "Morning sleep, midday wine, childish babbling, and attending the houses of assembly of the ignorant waste a man's life"[39].

15. R. Eleazar ha-Mudai said, "He who profanes things sacred, and despises the festivals, and puts his fellow-man to shame in public, and makes void the covenant of Abraham, our father[40], and makes the *Torah* bear a meaning other than the right[41]; (such a one) even

---

35. A contemporary of Jochanan ben Zakkai (10 B.C.E.-90 C.E.). See Friedlander, *Ben Dosa und seine Zeit* (Prag, 1872), and Bacher, *ibid.*, 283 *et seq.*
36. Cf. Ps. CXI, 10: "The beginning of wisdom is the fear of the Lord." "A man's fear of sin should be instinctive, rather than a result of calculation, . . . a man should build upon the foundation of religious feeling, rather than upon philosophy" (Taylor).
37. Cf. above, chapter I, 17, "Not learning but doing is the chief thing."
38. A contemporary of Jochanan ben Zakkai.
39. Idleness, etc., indispose one for the study of the *Torah* and for business.
40. *I.e.* circumcision.
41. Or "acts barefacedly against the *Torah*."

though knowledge of the *Torah* and good deeds be his, has no share in the world to come"[42].

16. R. Ishmael[43] said, "Be submissive to a superior[44], affable to the young[45], and receive all men with cheerfulness"[46].

17. R. Akiba[47] said, "Jesting and levity lead a man on to lewdness. The

---

42. Knowledge and moral excellence alone are not sufficient.
43. Lived about 120 C.E. See Bacher, *ibid.*, pp. 240-271.
44. Or "be pliant of disposition."
45. לטשחורת

is variously rendered as the "young" (Maimonides, Bartenors, Geigner, Jastrow), "impressment" (Rashbam, Taylor) "sovereign authority" (Levy, Child. Wörteburg, Fiebig) and "a suppliant" (Singer).
46. Cf. chapter I, 15.
47. Akiba ben Joseph (born about 50 C.E., died about 132) was the greatest of the *Tannaim* (teachers mentioned in the *Mishnah*). He was a "proselyte of righteousness" (*ger tzedek*). Until middle age, he remained illiterate and averse to study, but was spurred on to become learned in the *Torah* by the daughter of the rich Kalba Shabua, whom he subsequently married. He was the pupil of R. Eliezer ben Hyrcanos, R. Jochanan ben Chanania, and Nahum of Gimzo. He espoused the cause of Bar Kochba, acknowledging him as the Messiah, and is said to have travelled throughout the land stirring up opposition to Rome. At the fall of Betar, he was captured by the Romans, and most cruelly put to death, expiring with the *Shema* upon his lips. R. Akiba definitely fixed the canon of the Old Testament. He compiled and systematized the traditional law, in this respect being the forerunner of R. Judah ha-Nasi (see chapter II, n. 1), whose *Mishnah* may be considered as being derived from that of the school of Akiba. His importance may be gauged by the following statement from the *Talmud*, "Our *Mishnah* comes directly from R. Meïr (a disciple of Akiba), the *Tosefta* from R. Nehemiah, the *Sifra* from R. Judah, and the *Sifre* from R. Simon; but they all took Akiba for a model in their works and followed him" (*Sanhedrin*, 86a). Akiba introduced a new method of interpreting Scripture, in which not a word, syllable, or letter was considered superfluous, finding thereby a basis for many oral laws. His hermeneutical and exegetical activities were remarkable. Many interesting legends have clustered around his name. See Bacher, *ibid.*, 271-348; Meilziner, *Introduction to the Talmud*, pp. 29, 125-126; Isaacs, *Stories from the Rabbis*, p. 61 *et seq.*; Danziger, *ibid.*, pp. 152-184; the *Jewish Encyclopedia*, arts. *Akiba ben Joseph* and *Akiba ben Joseph in Legend;* Myers, *Story of the Jewish People*, pp. 171-188; and Geiger, *Judaism and its History*, p. 226 *et seq.*, 230 *et seq.*

Massorah[48] is a rampart around the *Torah*; tithes are a safeguard to riches[49]; good resolves are a fence to abstinence[50]; a hedge around wisdom is silence"[51].

18. He used to say, "Beloved is man, for he was created in the image (of God); but it was by a special love that it was made known to him that he was created in the image of God, as it is said, 'For in the image of God made he man'[52]. Beloved are Israel, or they were called children of the All-present, but it was by a special love that it was made known to them that they were called children of the All-present, as it is said, 'Ye are children unto the Lord your God'[53]. Beloved are Israel, for unto them was given the desirable instrument[54]; but it was by a special love that it was made known to them that that desirable instrument was theirs, through which the world was created, as it is said, 'For I give you good doctrine; forsake ye not my *Torah*'[55].

---

48. *Massorah*, from root *masar*, "to deliver," "hand over," "transmit," means a "chain of tradition." It is used to designate tradition in general, and is thus correlative with *kabbalah*. The *Massorah* contains information for the correct transcription of the Scripture. As used here, it means the traditional interpretation of the *Torah*. Cf. chapter I, 1, "Moses received the *Torah* on Sinai, and handed it down (*umsarah*) to Joshua," and "make a fence around the *Torah*." Consult Driver, *Notes on Samuel, Intro.*, p. 37 *et seq.*; Schurer, *ibid.*, II, i, 328; Taylor, *Sayings*, p. 55, n. 33; Friedlander *ibid.*, p. 55, 203, 266; *Jewish Encyclopedia* s.v.; and *The Companion Bible* (London, Oxford University Press), Pt. I, *Appendix*, 30.
49. On tithes, see chapter I, n. 37. Cf. *Shabbat*, 119a, and *Taanit*, 9a, "give tithes in order that thou mayest become rich."
50. Lit., "separation," *i.e.* from defilement, hence "sanctity" (Taylor).
51. Cf. chapter I, 17.
52. Gen. IX, 6.
53. Deut. XIV, 1.
54. *I.e.*, the *Torah*.
55. Prov. IV, 2.

19. Everything is foreseen, yet free will is given[56]; and the world is judged by grace, yet all is according to the amount of the work"[57].

20. He used to say, "Everything is given on pledge[58], and a net is spread for all living[59]; the shop is open[60]; the dealer gives credit; the ledger lies open; the hand writes; and whosoever wishes to borrow may come and borrow; but the collectors regularly make their daily round, and exact payment from man whether he be content or not[61]; and they have that whereon they can rely in their demand; and the judgment is a judgment of truth[62]; and everything is prepared for the feast"[63].

21. R. Eleazar, the son of Azariah [64], said, "Where there is no *Torah*, there are no manners; where there are no manners, there is no *Torah*: where there is no wisdom, there is no fear of God; where there is no fear of God, there is no wisdom: where there is no knowledge, there

---

56. The omniscience and prescience of God do not deprive men of free will. Maimonides explains this in the last chapter of the *Shemonah Perakim* (ed. Gorfinkle, p. 85 *et seq*.).
57. Maimonides interprets the last phrase as meaning to do many small deeds of charity rather than one great deed of goodness. For instance, it is better to distribute one hundred coins among one hundred people than to give them all to one person.
58. The world is compared to the office of a merchant.
59. Ecc. IX, 12: "for man also knoweth not his time, like the fishes that are caught in an evil net."
60. The shop stands for the world and its enjoyments.
61. Man has free will, and is therefore responsible for all his acts.
62. For everything is recorded.
63. This world is merely a preparation for the next. The enjoyment of the world to come is likened by the Rabbis to a banquet, which is shared in by the good and the bad, after they have paid off their moral debts.
64. R. Eleazar ben Azariah, a Mishnaic scholar of the first century, was of a rich and influential family, and was a descendent of Ezra the Scribe. At seventeen or eighteen, upon the deposition of Gamaliel II, Eleazar, because of his popularity and erudition, was chosen to fill the position of the president of the academy at Jabneh. Upon Gamaliel's restoration, he was made vice-president (*Ab bet din*). See Bacher, *ibid.*, 219-240.

no understanding; where there is no understanding, there is no knowledge⁶⁵: where there is no meal, there is no *Torah;* where there is no *Torah,* there is no meal"⁶⁶.

22. He used to say, "He whose wisdom exceeds his works, to what is he like? To a tree whose branches are many, but whose roots are few; and the wind comes and plucks it up, and overturns it upon its face, as it is said, 'And he shall be like a lonely juniper tree in the desert, and shall not see when good cometh; but shall inhabit the parched places in the wilderness, a salt land and not inhabited'⁶⁷. But he whose works exceed his wisdom, to what is he like? To a tree whose branches are few, but whose roots are many, so that though all the winds in the world come and blow upon it, they cannot stir it from its place, as it is said, 'And he shall be as a tree planted by the waters; and that spreadeth out its roots by the river and shall not perceive when heat cometh, but his leaf shall be green; and shall not be troubled in the year of drought, neither shall cease from yielding fruit'"⁶⁸.

23. R. Eleazar Chisma⁶⁹ said, "The laws concerning the sacrifices of birds and the purification of women are essential ordinances⁷⁰; astronomy and geometry are the after-courses of wisdom"⁷¹.

Rabbi Chanania, the son of Akashia, said, "The Holy One, blessed

---

65. Cf. Prov. IX, 10: "The fear of the Lord is the beginning of wisdom, and the knowledge of the holy is understanding."
66. Where there is a want of the means of sustenance there is no studying of *Torah,* and without spiritual nourishment, physical nourishment has no value.
67. Jer. XVII, 6.
68. Jer. XVII, 8. Cf. verse 12, above.
69. A contemporary of AKiba.
70. *Kinnim,* "nests," is the name of a tract in *Seder Kodashim* of the *Mishnah,* and tells of the young birds, which men and women were at times required to offer as sacrifice. *Niddah* is a tract of *Seder Teharot* of the *Mishnah,* and relates of the uncleannesses of woman.
71. *I.e.,* the mathematical sciences, in which R. Eleazar was very proficient, are only to be considered as helps to the study of the essentials of *Torah.*

be He, was pleased to make Israel worthy; wherefore He gave them a copious *Torah* and many commandments, as it is said, 'It pleased the Lord, for his righteousness' sake, to magnify the *Torah* and make it honorable'".

CHAPTER
FOUR

All Israel[1] have a portion in the world to come, and it is said, "And thy people shall be all righteous; they shall inherit the land for ever, the branch of my planting, the work of my hands, that I may be glorified".

1. Ben Zoma[2] said, "Who is wise? He who learns from all men, as it is

---

1. The original text featured the lines "All Israel," etc., on page 29, both as the opening and closing lines of each chapter, with the page numbers marking the start and end of Chapter I. Instead of citing these sentences in the same manner, this version places them directly where they belong within the text. The editor feels that this approach more accurately preserves the essence of the original material
2. Simon ben Zoma and Simon ben Azzai, *Tannaim* of the second century, were generally known as ben Zoma and ben Azzai, as they never received the title of Rabbi, according to one view. According to another opinion, they were called by their fathers' names, because they both died young. Together with Akiba and Elisha ben Abuyah (*Acher*), they entered, legend says, into the paradise of esoteric knowledge. "Four (sages)," we are told, "entered paradise, ben Azzai, ben Zoma, Acher, and Akiba. Ben Azzai looked and died; ben Zoma went mad; Acher destroyed the plants; Akiba alone came out unhurt" (*Chagigah*, 14b). The interpretation of this passage is that ben Azzai died prematurely, worn out by his activities in mystical and theosophic speculation; ben Zoma became demented thereby; Elisha, contemptuously referred to as Acher

said, 'from all my teachers have I gotten understanding'³. Who is mighty? He who controls his passions, as it is said, 'He that is slow to anger is better than the mighty, and he that ruleth over his spirit than he that taketh a city'⁴. Who is rich? He who rejoices in his portion, as it is said, 'When thou eatest the labor of thine hands, happy art thou, and it shall be well with thee'⁵; happy art thou in this world,⁶ and it shall be well with thee in the world to come. Who is honored? He who honors others, as it is said, 'For them that honor me I will honor, and they that despise me shall be held in contempt'"⁷.

2. Ben Azzai⁸ said, "Hasten to do even a slight precept⁹, and flee from transgression; for one virtue leads to another, and transgression draws transgression in its train; for the recompense of a virtue is a virtue, and the recompense of a transgression is a transgression"¹⁰.

(the other), became an apostate; but Akiba was unaffected. Ben Zoma was famous for his wisdom, it being said of him, "Whoever sees ben Zoma in his dream is assured of scholarship" (*Berachot*, 57b). With him, it was said, the last of the interpreters of the Law (*darshanim*) died (*Sotah*, 49b). His interpretation of the biblical passage "that thou mayest remember when thou camest forth out of Egypt" is found in the *Haggadah* of Passover eve. See Bacher, *Agada der Tanaiten*, pp. 425-532; Schechter, *Studies*, I, pp. 129-130; H. Sperling, in *Aspects of the Hebrew Genius*, p. 150.

3. Ps. CXIX, 9.
4. Prov. XVI, 32.
5. Ps. CXXVIII, 2. The discontented rich man, even, is poor.
6. The editor corrected the error in the source text where the comma after "world" was a period.
7. I Sam. II, 30.
8. Simon ben Azzai (see n. 1) was a very assiduous student and a man of great piety. He was betrothed to the daughter of Akiba, but separated from his prospective wife in order to devote all of his time to study. It was said of him, "At the death of ben Azzai, the last industrious man passed away" (*Sotah* IX, 15), and "He who sees ben Azzai in a dream might hope for saintliness." He declared that the greatest principle of Judaism is the belief in the common brotherhood of all mankind, which he derived from the passage, Genesis VI, 1, "This is the generation of Adam (man)." See Bacher, *ibid.*, 409-424.
9. Cf. chapter II, 1.
10. Well-doing is the fruit of well-doing, and evil-doing the fruit of evil-doing.

3. He used to say, "Despise not any man, and carp not at any thing[11]; for there is not a man that has not his hour, and there is not a thing that has not its place."

4. R. Levitas of Jabneh said, "Be exceedingly lowly of spirit[12], since the hope of man is but the worm."

5. R. Jochanan, the son of Berokah[13], said, "Whosoever profanes the Name of Heaven[14] in secret will suffer the penalty for it in public; and this, whether the Heavenly Name be profaned in ignorance or in wilfulness."

6. R. Ishmael[15], his son, said, "He who learns in order to teach[16], to him the means will be granted both to learn and to teach; but he who learns in order to practise, to him the means will be granted to learn, and to teach, to observe, and to practise."

---

11. Or "do not consider anything as being impossible."
12. R. Levitas lived probably about 120 C.E. Maimonides declares that the medium way between the extremes of the *too little* and the *too much* is the path of virtue, but he makes an exception in the case of humility, and, in accordance with this passage, considers the extreme of being very humble the virtue. See Gorfinkle, *The Eight Chapters*, p. 60, n. 2.
13. A contemporary of Akiba.
14. "Name of Heaven" is a common substitute for the "name of God."
15. He lived about 150 C.E.
16. To one who learns *Torah* and does not teach it are applied the words in Num. XV, 31: "he hath despised the word of the Lord" (*Sanhedrin*, 99a).

7. R. Zadok said, "Separate not thyself from the congregation; (in the judge's office) act not the counsel's part[17]; make not of the *Torah* a crown wherewith to aggrandize thyself, nor a spade wherewith to dig"[18]. So also used Hillel to say, "He who makes a worldly use of the crown (of the *Torah*) shall waste away"[19]. Hence thou mayest infer that whosoever derives a profit for himself from the words of the *Torah* is helping on his own destruction.

8. R. Jose[20] said, "Whoso honors the *Torah* will himself be honored by mankind, but whoso dishonors the *Torah* will himself be dishonored by mankind."

9. R. Ishmael[21], his son, said, "He who shuns the judicial office rids himself of hatred, robbery, and vain swearing[22]; but he who presumptuously lays down decisions is foolish, wicked, and of an arrogant spirit."

10. He used to say, "Judge not alone, for none may judge alone save One; neither say (to thy judicial colleagues), 'Accept my view,' for the choice is theirs (to concur); and it is not for thee (to compel concurrence)."

---

17. Cf. chapter I, 8.
18. *I.e.*, for material and selfish ends.
19. Cf. chapter I, 13.
20. R. Jose ben Chalafta was a contemporary of R. Meïr.
21. He lived about 160-220 C.E.
22. The judge brings upon himself the hatred of the one who is disappointed by his judgment. An erroneous judgment is equivalent to robbery. When the judge exacts an unnecessary oath, perjury may result.

11. R. Jonathan[23] said, "Whoso fulfils the *Torah* in the midst of poverty shall in the end fulfil it in the midst of wealth; and whoso neglects the *Torah* in the midst of wealth shall in the end neglect it in the midst of poverty."

12. R. Meïr[24] said, "Lessen thy toil for worldly goods, and be busy in the *Torah*; be humble of spirit before all men; if thou neglectest the *Torah*, many causes for neglecting it will be present themselves to thee, but if thou laborest in the *Torah*, He has abundant recompense to give thee."

13. R. Elieser[25], the son of Jacob, said, "He who does one precept has gotten himself one advocate; and he who commits one transgression has gotten himself one accuser. Repentance and good deeds are as a shield against punishment."

14. R. Jochanan, the sandal-maker[26], said, "Every assembly which is

---

23. He lived about the middle of the second century C.E. He was a pupil of R. Ishmael (verse 9).
24. See chapter III, n. 32.
25. He lived about 140 C.E.
26. Most of the Rabbis believed with Rabban Gamaliel that the study of the *Torah* without employment brings transgression (chapter II, 2). Consequently, each invariably followed some vocation. Hillel, the senior, gained his livelihood as a wood-chopper; Shammai was a builder; R. Joshua, a blacksmith; R. Chanina, a shoemaker; R. Huna, a water-carrier; R. Abba, a tailor; R. Pappa, a brewer, etc. Other Rabbis whose names indicate their trades, as R. Jochanan ha-Sandalar (lived about 150 C.E.), were Isaac Nappacha (the smith) and R. Abin Naggara (the carpenter). Many were merchants and others agriculturists. Generally, the Rabbi studied during two-thirds of the day, and worked at his trade during the remainder. Those engaged in agriculture would study in the winter and till the soil in the summer. Consult Franz Delitzch, *Jewish Artisan Life in the Time of Christ*; and S. Meyer, *Arbeit und Handwerk im Talmud*, Berlin, 1878.

in the Name of Heaven will in the end be established, but that which is not in the Name of Heaven will not in the end be established."

15. R. Eleazer, the son of Shammua[27], said, "Let the honor of thy disciple be as dear to thee as thine own, and the honor of thine associate be like the fear of thy master, and the fear of thy master like the fear of Heaven."

16. R. Judah[28] said, "Be cautious in study, for an error in study may amount to presumptuous sin"[29].

17. R. Simeon[30] said, "There are three crowns: the crown of *Torah*, the crown of priesthood, and the crown of royalty; but the crown of a good name excels them all."

18. R. Nehorai[31] said, "Betake thyself to a home of the *Torah*[32], and say not that the *Torah* will come after thee; for there thy associates will establish thee in the possession of it; and lean not upon thine own understanding"[33].

---

27. He lived about 150 C.E.
28. R. Judah ben Ilai lived about 140 C.E.
29. Cf. Chapter III, 10.
30. On R. Simeon ben Yochai, see chapter III, n. 12.
31. He lived about 130 C.E.
32. If there is no teacher where you live.
33. Prov. III, 5.

19. R. Jannia said, "It is not in our power (to explain) either the prosperity of the wicked or the afflictions of the righteous."

20. R. Mattithiah, the son of Heresh[34], said, "Be beforehand in the salutation of peace to all men; and be rather a tail to lions than a head to foxes"[35].

21. R. Jacob[36] said, "This world is like a vestibule before the world to come[37]; prepare thyself in the vestibule, that thou mayest enter into the hall." 22. He used to say, "Better is one hour of repentance and good deeds in this world than the whole life of the world to come; and better is one hour of blissfulness of spirit in the world to come than the whole life of this world."

23. R. Simeon, the son of Eleazer[38], said, "Do not appease thy fellow in the hour of his anger, and comfort him not in the hour when his dead lies before him, and question him not in the hour of his vow, and rush not to see him in the hour of his disgrace."

24. Samuel[39], the younger, used to say, "Rejoice not when thine

---

34. He lived about 120 C.E. in Rome.
35. It is better to be a pupil of great teachers than to be a teacher of worthless pupils (Maimonides). It is better to follow those who are greater than to lead those who are inferior.
36. He lived about 160-220 C.E.
37. This world is a bridge that leads to the future world (Maimonides).
38. A pupil of R. Meïr. He lived about 160-220 C.E.
39. Samuel (about 120 C.E.) is said to have composed, at the request of R. Gamaliel II, the prayer against heretics, added to the "Eighteen Benedictions" (*Shemoneh Esreh*). See the *Jewish Encyclopedia*, vol. XI, p. 281.

enemy falleth, and let not thine heart be glad when he stumbleth: lest the Lord see it and it displease him, and he turn away his wrath from him"[40].

25. Elisha, the son of Abuyah[41], said, "If one learns as a child, what is it like? Like ink written in clean paper. If one learns as an old man, what is it like? Like ink written on used paper"[42].

26. R. Jose, the son of Judah[43], of Chefar Babli said, "He who learns from the young, to what is he like? To one who eats unripe grapes,

---

40. Prov. XXIV, 17, 18.
41. See n. 1, above. Elisha ben Abuyah, otherwise known as Acher, lived at the end of the first and the beginning of the second century. He is charged by the Rabbis with having aided the Romans in their attempts to suppress the Jewish religion, with having endeavored to estrange the young from Judaism and from the study of its literature, with having intentionally and openly broken the ceremonial laws, and with having desecrated the Sabbath. R. Meïr, his pupil, maintained a close intimacy with him, in spite of his apostasy, having high regard for Elisha's intellectual worth. When reproached for this, R. Meïr said, "I eat the kernel, and throw away the husks." Elisha is often referred to as the "Faust of the *Talmud*." On his identification with the Apostle Paul, see I. M. Wise, *The Origin of Christianity*, p. 311, and Danziger, *ibid.*, pp. 304-306. Some have even identified him with Jesus. In *Abot de-Rabbi Natan*, a parable that is very similar to that of Jesus, in Luke VI 47-49, is attributed to Elisha. "A man who does good deeds and diligently studies the Law, to whom is he likened? He is like a man building a house with a stone foundation and with tiles (on the roof); and when a flood arises, and breaks against the walls, that house cannot be moved from its place. But the man who lives an evil life, in spite of having deeply studied the Law, to whom is he like? He is like a man building a house with tiles for a foundation and with heavy stones (on the roof); and when a little rain comes, straightway the house falls in" (G. Friedlander's translation, in *The Jewish Sources of the Sermon on the Mount*, pp. 259-260). On the career of Acher, see Bacher, *ibid.*, pp. 432-436; Graetz, *History*, II, *passim*; Myers, *ibid.*, pp. 200-202; and Strack, *Einleitung in den Talmud*, p. 91.
42. What one learns in youth, one retains, while the opposite is true of learning in old age. The Rabbis, elsewhere, liken learning in youth to engraving upon a stone, and learning in old age to writing on the sand.
43. A contemporary of Judah ha-Nasi.

and drinks wine from his vat[44]. And he who learns from the old, to what is he like? To one who eats ripe grapes, and drinks old wine."

27. Rabbi Meïr said[45], "Look not at the flask, but at what it contains: there may be a new flask full of old wine, and an old flask that has not even new wine in it"[46].

28. R. Eleazar ha-Kappar[47] said, "Envy, cupidity, and ambition take a man from the world"[48].

29. He used to say, "They that are born are doomed to die; and the dead to be brought to life again; and the living to be judged, to know, to make known, and to be made conscious that He is God, He the Maker, He the Creator, He the Discerner[49], He the Judge, He the Witness[50], He the Accuser; He it is that will in future judge, blessed be He, with Whom there is no unrighteousness, nor forgetfulness, nor respect of persons, nor taking of bribes[51]; and know also that

---

44. *I.e.*, wine that is not forty days old, and not yet clarified.
45. Some texts read "Rabbi," *i.e.*, Judah ha-Nasi (see chapter II, n. 1).
46. This verse expresses an opinion contrary to that of the preceding one. The mind of a young man may be more mature than that of an old man.
47. A contemporary of Judah ha-Nasi.
48. Cf. chapter II, 16.
49. Cf. Ps. XXXIII, 15: "He fashioneth their hearts altogether; he hath regard to all their works."
50. Cf. Mal. III, 5.
51. Cf. II Chron. XIX, 7: "Take heed and act; for with the Lord our God there is no injustice, nor respect for persons, nor taking of bribes." Maimonides interprets this verse of *Abot* as meaning that one cannot bribe God with good deeds in order to have bad deeds forgiven. The one bad deed is not forgiven even by the doing of one hundred good ones, but punishment is meted out for the bad deed and reward in full for the hundred good ones. That is, each action is judged entirely on its own merits. Neither is God a respecter of persons. On the one hand, He punished Moses for his anger at the

everything is according to the reckoning[52]; and let not thy imagination give thee hope that the grave will be a place of refuge for thee; for perforce thou wast formed, and perforce thou wast born, and thou livest perforce, and perforce thou wilt die, and perforce thou wilt in the future have to give account and reckoning before the Supreme King of kings, the Holy One, blessed be He."

Rabbi Chanania, the son of Akashia, said, "The Holy One, blessed be He, was pleased to make Israel worthy; wherefore He gave them a copious *Torah* and many commandments, as it is said, 'It pleased the Lord, for his righteousness' sake, to magnify the *Torah* and make it honorable'".

---

waters of Meribah, and, on the other, He rewarded Esau for honoring his parents, and Nebuchadnezzar for honoring God.

52. Maimonides interprets as follows, "Think of the physical things in which man has no choice, as our sages said, 'All is in the power of God, except the fear of God.' It is not said that one must perforce, and against one's will, sin, or that one is constrained to journey, walk, stand, etc., for these are in the power of man, and are dependent upon his own free will, and not upon any (external) compelling force, as we have explained in chapter eight." See Rawicz, *Commentar des Maimonides*, p. 89, n. 4, and Garfinkle, *ibid.*, p. 88 *et seq.*

CHAPTER
FIVE

All Israel have a portion in the world to come, and it is said, "And thy people shall be all righteous; they shall inherit the land for ever, the branch of my planting, the work of my hands, that I may be glorified".

1. With ten sayings the world was created. What does this teach us? Could it not have been created with one saying? It is to make known the punishment that will befall the wicked who destroy the world that was created with ten sayings, as well as the goodly reward that will be bestowed upon the just who preserve the world that was created with ten sayings[1].

---

1. The expression "and God said" occurs ten times in Genesis I (verses 3, 6, 9, 11, 14, 20, 24, 26 28, and 29). Many commentators count the opening phrase of this chapter, "In the beginning God created the heavens and the earth," as one of the sayings, maintaining that the idea of saying is implied in it. Cf. Ps. XXXIII, 16. According to the Rabbis, the wicked destroy and the righteous preserve the world, and, since it required ten sayings to create the world, the guilt of the sinner and the righteousness of the just are emphasized more than if it had been created merely by one word.

2. There were ten generations from Adam to Noah, to make known how long-suffering God is, seeing that all those generations continued provoking him, until he brought upon them the waters of the flood[2].

3. There were ten generations from Noah to Abraham, to make known how long-suffering God is, seeing that all those generations continued provoking him, until Abraham, our father, came, and received the reward they should all have earned[3].

4. With ten trials our father Abraham was tried[4], and he stood firm in them all, to make known how great was the love of our father Abraham[5].

---

2. The ten generations are Adam, Seth, Enosh, Kenan, Mahalalel, Jared, Enoch, Methusaleh, Lamech, and Noah. The period from Adam to Noah is known as the "generation of the flood" (*dor ha-mabbul*).
3. These are Shem, Arpachshad, Shelah, Eber, Peleg, Reu, Serug, Nahor, Terah, and Abraham. Noah's good deeds were sufficient only to save himself and family, while Abraham's were sufficient to sustain the whole world.
4. These trials may be reckoned as follows: (1) his migration, Gen. XII, 12; (2) the famine in Canaan, XII, 10; (3) the seizing of Sarah by Pharaoh, XII, 15; (4) the battle with the four kings, XIV; (5) his marriage with Hagar because of Sarah's sterility, XVI, 2; (6) the circumcision, XVII, 10; (7) the seizing of Sarah by Abimelech, king of Gerar, XX, 2; (8) the banishment of Hagar, XXI, 10; (9) the banishment of Ishmael, XXI, 10; and (10) God's command to sacrifice Isaac, XXII, 2. See *Pirke de-Rabbi Eliezer*, chapter 24, and Friedlander, G., *Rabbinic philosophy and Ethics* (London, 1912), p. 75, n. 4.
5. For God. Some interpreters explain this, however, as "the love of God for Abraham."

5. Ten miracles were wrought for our fathers in Egypt[6], and ten at the Sea[7].

6. Ten plagues did the Holy One, blessed be He, bring upon the Egyptians in Egypt, and ten at the Sea[8].

7. With ten temptations did our fathers tempt the Holy One, blessed be He, in the wilderness, as it is said, "And they tempted me these ten times, and have not hearkened to my voice"[9].

8. Ten miracles were wrought for our fathers in the Temple; no woman miscarried from the scent of the holy flesh; the holy flesh never became putrid; no fly[10] was seen in the slaughter-house; no unclean accident ever befell the high-priest on the Day of Atonement; the rain never quenched the fire of the wood-pile on the altar[11]; neither did the wind overcome the column of smoke that arose therefrom[12]; nor was there ever found any disqualifying defect in the

---

6. That they escaped the ten plagues with which the Egyptians were afflicted.

7. Legend says that at the passage of the Red Sea the ten miracles wrought were as follows: (1) the waters divided; (2) the waters were like a tent, or a vault; (3) the sea-bed was dry and hard; (4) but when the Egyptians trod upon it, it became muddy and slimy; (5) the sea was divided into twelve parts, one for each tribe; (6) the waters became as hard as stone; (7) the congealed waters appeared like blocks of building-stone; (8) the water was transparent so that the tribes could see one another; (9) fresh drinking water flowed from the congealed water; (10) after Israel had partaken of the drinking water, it became congealed, and did not wet the ground under foot. See Ginzberg, *Legends of the Jews*, III, p. 21 *et seq.*

8. This verse is not found in the Talmudic versions of *Abot*. The plagues at the sea are alluded to in the "Song of Moses," Ex. XV. See the commentary of Bartenora.

9. Num. XIV, 22. The ten are enumerated by Maimonides, Bartenora, Hoffmann, and others.

10. The fly is a symbol of impurity.

11. The altar stood in the midst of the roofless Temple-hall.

12. The straight column of smoke denoted the acceptance of prayer and sacrifice.

omer (of new barley, offered on the second day of Passover) or in the two loaves (the first fruits of the wheat-harvest, offered on Pentecost)[13], or in the shewbread[14]; though the people stood closely pressed together, they found ample space to prostrate themselves; never did serpent or scorpion injure any one in Jerusalem; nor did any man ever say to his fellow, "the place is too strait for me[15] to lodge over night in Jerusalem."

9. Ten things were created on the eve of Sabbath in the twilight[16]: the mouth of the earth[17]; the mouth of the well[18]; the mouth of the ass[19]; the rainbow[20]; the manna[21]; the rod[22]; the shamir[23]; the shape of written characters; the writing, and the tables of stone: some say, the destroying spirits also, and the sepulchre of Moses[24], and the ram of Abraham our father[25]; and others say, tongs, also, made with tongs[26].

---

13. See Lev. XXIII, 15-17.
14. Every Sabbath, twelve loaves of bread were placed on a table in the Sanctuary "before the Lord" (Lev. XXIV, 5-9) to serve as a constant reminder to the twelve tribes that their place was before the altar of God.
15. Isa. XLIX, 20.
16. Since all things were said to have been created during the first six days of creation, and since "there is nothing new under the sun" (Eccles. I, 9), everything miraculous or supernatural that existed or occurred after creation was explained by the Rabbis as having been made or preordained in the twilight at the moment of transition between the end of the work of creation and the beginning of the Sabbath. See Gorfinkle, *ibid.*, pp. 90-91 and n. 1.
17. To swallow Korah and his followers. See Num. XVI, 30.
18. Which supplied the Israelites with water during their wandering in the wilderness. See Num. XXI, 16, and *Shabbat*, 35a.
19. Balaam's ass. See Num. XXII, 28.
20. Ge. IX, 19.
21. Ex. XV, 16.
22. Of Moses. See *ibid.*, IV, 17.
23. A miraculous worm that split stones by its look. It was used, according to legend, to engrave the names of the tribes on the jewels of the ephod of the high-priest, and was also employed by Solomon in the construction of the Temple, in which no tools of iron were used. See *Gittin*, 68a, and *Sotah*, 48b. Consult P. Cassel, *Shamir, ein archaol. Beitrag zur Natur und Sagenkunde*, Erfurt, 1856, and art. *Shamir*, in *Jewish Encyclopedia*.
24. Deut. XXXIV, 6.
25. Gen. XXII, 13.
26. An allusion to a saying found in *Tosefta Erubin*, "Tongs are made with tongs; but

10. There are seven marks of an uncultured, and seven of a wise man. The wise man does not speak before him who is greater than he in wisdom; and does not interrupt the speech of his companion; he is not hasty to answer; he questions according to the subject-matter; and answers to the point; he speaks upon the first thing first, and upon the last, last; regarding that which he has not understood he says, "I do not understand it;" and he acknowledges the truth. The reverse of all this is to be found in an uncultured man.

11. Seven kinds of punishment come into the world for seven important transgressions. If some give their tithes[27] and others do not, a dearth ensues from drought and some suffer hunger while others are full. If they all determine to give no tithes, a dearth ensures from tumult[28] and drought. If they further resolve not to give the dough-cake[29], an exterminating dearth ensures. Pestilence comes into the world to fulfil those death penalties threatened in the *Torah*, the execution of which, however, is within the function of a human tribunal[30], and for the violation of the law regarding the

---

how was the first pair made? It could only have been a creation of God." One instrument presupposes another; one thing is the cause of another, but the original cause is God. Cf. *Pesachim*, 54a.

27. See chapter I, n. 37.
28. Of war, when agriculture is neglected, and crops are destroyed, etc.
29. Num. XV, 20: "Ye shall offer up a cake of the first of your dough for a heave offering." This commandment is observed in spirit to-day by the Jewish housewife, who takes a part of bread which is kneaded, and burns it, after reciting the blessing, "Blessed art Thou, O Lord, our God, King of the universe, Who has sanctified us by Thy commandments, and commanded us to separate the *challah*." The ninth treatise of the *Order Zeraim* of the *Mishnah* is called *Challah*. See Friedlander, *Jewish Religion*, p. 357.
30. The execution of which is in the hands of God.

fruits of the seventh year[31]. The sword[32] comes into the world for the delay of justice, and for the perversion of justice, and on account of the offence of those who interpret the *Torah*, not according to its true sense[33]. Noxious beasts come into the world for vain swearing[34], and for the profanation of the Divine Name[35]. Captivity comes into the world on account of idolatry, immortality, bloodshed, and the neglect of the year of rest for the soil.

12. At four periods pestilence grows apace: in the fourth year, in the seventh, at the conclusion of the seventh year, and at the conclusion of the Feast of Tabernacles in each year: in the fourth year, for default of giving the tithe to the poor in the third year[36]; in the seventh year, for default of giving the title to the poor in the sixth year[37]; at the conclusion of the seventh year, for the violation of the law regarding the fruits of the seventh year (31), and at the conclusion of the Feast of Tabernacles in each year, for robbing the poor of the grants legally assigned to them[38].

13. There are four characters among men: he who says, "What is mine is mine and what is thine is thine," his is a neutral character;

---

31. That is, the Sabbatical year or the year of release (*ha-shemittah*). See Ex. XXIII, 10 *et seq.*, and Lev. XXV, 1-7. It is commanded that the land be allowed to lie fallow during that year, that there be no sowing, nor reaping, nor pruning of the vineyards, and that the servants, strangers, and animals, as well as the owner, shall share in the spontaneous growth of the fields and the vineyards. See also Deut. XV, 1-11, and *Tractate Shebiit* of the *Mishnah*.
32. *I.e.*, war.
33. By prohibiting the permissible and permitting the prohibited.
34. Cf. chapter IV, 9.
35. Cf. chapter IV, 5.
36. See Deut. XIV, 28, 29; XXVI, 12, and also above, chapter I, n. 37.
37. Of the septennial cycle. The tithe was to be brought at the end of *every* three years.
38. *I.e.*, the gleanings and the forgotten sheaves of the harvest, the single bunches of grapes of the vineyard, and the unreaped corners of the fields which were assigned to the stranger, the fatherless, and the widow.

some say, "This is a character like that of Sodom"[39]; he who says, "What is mine is thine and what is thine is mine," is a boor[40]; he who says, "What is mine is thine and what is thine is thine," is a saint; he who says, "What is thine is mine and what is mine is mine," is a wicked man.

14. There are four kinds of tempers: he whom it is easy to provoke and easy to pacify, his loss disappears in his gain; he whom it is hard to provoke and hard to pacify, his gain disappears in his loss; he whom it is hard to provoke and easy to pacify is a saint; he whom it is easy to provoke and hard to pacify is a wicked man.

15. There are four qualities in disciples: he who quickly understands and quickly forgets, his gain disappears in his loss; he who understands with difficulty and forgets with difficulty, his loss disappears in his gain; he who understands quickly and forgets with difficulty, his is a good portion; he who understands with difficulty and forgets quickly, his is an evil portion.

16. As to almsgiving there are four dispositions: he who desires to give, but that others should not give, his eye is evil toward what appertains to others[41]; he who desires that others should give, but will not give himself, his eye is evil against what is his own; he who gives and wishes others to give is a saint; he who will not give and does not wish others to give is a wicked man.

---

39. One who neither gives nor takes. One who does no labor of love. Cf. Ezek. XVI, 49.
40. He does not know the sacredness of the rights of property.
41. He does not want his neighbors to be blessed because of their liberality.

17. There are four characters among those who attend the house of study: he who goes and does not practise[42] secures the reward for going; he who practises[43] but does not go secures the reward for practising; he who goes and practises is a saint; he who neither goes nor practises is a wicked man.

18. There are four qualities among those that sit before the wise: they are like a sponge, a funnel, a strainer, or a sieve: a sponge, which sucks up everything[44]; a funnel, which lets in at one end and out at the other; a strainer, which lets the wine pass out and retains the dregs; a sieve, which lets out the bran and retains the fine flour.

19. Whenever love depends upon some material cause, with the passing away of that cause, the love, too, passes away[45]; but if it be not depending upon such a cause, it will not pass away for ever. Which love was that which depended upon a material cause? Such was the love of Ammon and Tamar[46]. And that which depended upon no such cause? Such was the love of David and Jonathan[47].

20. Every controversy that is in the Name of Heaven[48] shall in the end lead to a permanent result, but every controversy that is not in the Name of Heaven shall not lead to a permanent result. Which controversy was that which was in the Name of Heaven? Such was the

---

42. The duties of which he has learned.
43. The commands of the *Torah*.
44. The true and the untrue.
45. Lasting love is disinterested love.
46. See II Sam. XII.
47. See I Sam. XVIII, 1.
48. *I.e.*, a controversy to arrive at the truth.

controversy of Hillel and Shammai[49]. And that which was not in the Name of Heaven? Such was the controversy of Korah and all his company[50].

21. Whosoever causes the multitude to be righteous, over him sin prevails not; but he who causes the multitude to sin shall not have the means to repent[51]. Moses was righteous and made the multitude righteous; the righteousness of the multitude was laid upon him, as it is said, "He executed the justice of the Lord and his judgments with Israel"[52]. Jeroboam, the son of Nebat, sinned and caused the multitude to sin; the sin of the multitude was laid upon him, as it is said, "For the sins of Jeroboam which he sinned and which he made Israel to sin"[53].

22. Whosoever has these three attributes is of the disciples of Abraham, our father, but whosoever has three other attributes is of the disciples of Balaam, the wicked[54]. A good eye[55], a humble mind, and a lowly spirit (are the tokens) of the disciples of Abraham, our

---

49. See chapter I, n. 29.
50. See Num. XV, 1 *et seq.*
51. He who leads the people astray is punished by being prevented from repenting. This does not mean, however, that man, in general, does not act in accordance with his own free will. Maimonides, in discussing this problem, says, in the eighth chapter of the *Shemonah Perakim*, "Just as some of man's undertakings, which are ordinarily subject to his own free will, are frustrated by way of punishment, as, for instance, a man's hand being prevented from working so that he can do nothing with it, as was the case of Jeroboam, the son of Nebat, or a man's eyes from seeing, as happened to the Sodomites, who had assembled about Lot, likewise how does God withhold man's ability to use his own free will in regard to repentance, so that it never occurs to him to repent, and he thus finally perishes in his own wickedness." See ed. Gorfinkle, p. 94 *et seq.*
52. Deut. XXXIII, 21.
53. I Kings XV, 30. Cf. *Sanhedrin* X, 2: "Three kings have no portion in the world to come... Jeroboam, Ahab, and Manasseh."
54. See Num. XXII-XXIV.
55. See chapter II, note 30.

father; an evil eye, a haughty mind, and a proud spirit (are the signs) of the disciples of Balaam, the wicked. What is the difference between the disciples of Abraham, our father, and those of Balaam, the wicked? The disciples of Abraham, our father, enjoy this world and inherit the world to come, as it is said, "That I may cause those that love me to inherit substance, and may fill all their treasuries"[56]; but the disciples of Balaam, the wicked, inherit *Gehinnom*[57], and descend into the pit of destruction, as it is said, "But thou, O God, wilt bring them down into the pit of destruction; bloodthirsty and deceitful men shall not live out half their days; but I will trust in thee"[58].

23. Judah, the son of Tema, said, "Be bold as a leopard, swift as an eagle, fleet as a hart, and strong as a lion, to do the will of thy Father who is in Heaven"[59].

---

56. Prov. VIII, 21: "Substance," *i.e.*, in the future world; "treasures," *i.e.*, in this world.
57. See chapter I, n. 18.
58. Ps. LIV, 24.
59. Cf. "Our Father which is in Heaven" of the "Lord's Prayer" (Matt. VI, 9). The conception of God as a "Father" goes back to earliest times. See Gen. XLIX, 19, 20; Ex. IV, 22; Deut. XXXII, 6; II Sam. V, 44; Ps. LXXXIX, 27, 28; Isa. LXIII, 16, LXIV, 8, and Mal. II, 10. Deut. XXXII, 6, reads, "Is He not thy Father?" and Isa. LXIII, 18, "Doubtless Thou art our Father." In the *Mishnah* we find, "Who purifies you? Your Father which is in Heaven" (*Yoma* VII, 8); "On whom have we to lean? On our Father which is in Heaven" (*Sotah*, IX, 15), and similar passages. The Rabbis constantly referred to God as "Father" (see Schechter, *Aspects*, pp. 46, 49, 50-51). They took issue, of course, with the New Testament conception of God, in not admitting and in denouncing the idea of a mediator. To them all mankind were the sons of God. That the Rabbis borrowed this God-idea and the expression "Our Father which is in Heaven" from Christianity is untenable, for, as Herford (*Pharisaism*, 120 *et seq.*) points out, such borrowing would have been abhorrent to them. This expression was undoubtedly current long before and during the time of Jesus, and it represented a conception of the divine acceptable to both the Rabbis and Jesus. The Rabbis had no quarrel with Christianity on this score, but did not admit the "sonship" of God in the Christian sense. The expressions "Our Father" and "Our Father which is in Heaven" are found frequently in the Jewish Prayer-book. On this subject, consult Taylor, *Sayings*, pp. 124, 176, and G. Friedlander, *The Jewish Sources of the Sermon on the Mount*, chapter X. For a comparison of other parts of *Abot* with the New Testament see Feibig, *Pirque 'aboth*, especially the *Nachwort*, pp. 42-43, and G. Friedlander, *ibid.*, *passim*. It seems that originally *Abot* ended here, as in the *Machzor Vitry*. The verses which follow were added from other sources.

24. He used to say[60], "At five years (the age is reached for the study of the) Scripture, at ten for (the study of) the *Mishnah*[61], at thirteen for (the fulfilment of) the commandments[62], at fifteen for (the study of) the *Talmud*[63], at eighteen for marriage, at twenty for seeking (a liveli-

---

See Bacher, *Agada der Tanaiten*, I, 378; Taylor, *ibid.*, p. 95, n. 46, p. 96, n. 47; Hoffmann, *Die erste Mischna*, p. 30; *idem*, *Abot*, p. 358, notes 106 and 108; and Strack, *Spruche*, p. 46, notes *t* and *u*.

60. Taylor makes this verse an *addendum* to chapter V, and calls it "The Ages of Man." Cf. Shakespeare's "Seven Ages of Man." See in the *Jewish Encyclopedia*, art. *Ages of Man in Jewish Literature, The Seven*, and Schechter, *Studies*, I, pp. 299-300.

61. The *Mishnah* is the oral or unwritten law based on the written law contained in the Pentateuch (see chapter I, n. 1). The *Mishnah*, *par excellence*, is the codification made by Judah ha-Nasi (see chapter II, n. 1). It is divided into six orders or sections known as *sedarim*. They are (1) *Zeraim*, "seeds," which contains the laws regarding the cultivation of the land and its products, introduced by a treatise concerning prayer and benedictions (*Berachot*); (2) *Mode*, "festivals," treating of the laws of the Sabbath and the festivals; (3) *Nashim*, "women," regulations concerning marriage and divorce; (4) *Nezikin*, "injuries" or "damages," civil and criminal law; (5) *Kodashim*, "holy things," the laws of sacrifice and of the service of the Temple; and (6) *Tohorot*, "purifications," dealing with the clean and the unclean. Each order is subdivided into treatises (*massektot*), there being in all 63 such subdivisions. The *Mishnah* is known as the *shas* (ש"ס), which word is formed from the first letters of the words *shishah sedarim* (six orders). The *Talmud* is also similarly termed. For a discussion of the name, origin, contents, compilation, etc., of the *Mishnah*, see Mielziner, *Introduction to the Talmud*, p. 4 *et seq.*; art. *Mishnah*, in the *Jewish Encyclopedia* and the authorities cited there; Strack, *Einleitung*, p. 2, 15 *et seq.*, 22 *et seq.*, and Geiger, *Judaism and its History*, p. 239 *et seq.*

62. At thirteen, the Jewish boy becomes *bar mitzwah*, i.e., "a son of commandment." The rites and ceremonies connected with the *bar mitzwah* of to-day cannot "be clearly traced earlier than the fourteenth century" (Abrahams, *Jewish Life in the Middle Ages*, p. 32). See Schurer, *History*, II, ii, p. 53 and n. 38; Schechter, *Studies*, I, p. 306 *et seq.*, and art. *Bar Mitzwah*, in *Jewish Encyclopedia*.

63. Lit., "teaching," "learning," "study." Here, it signifies study for the purpose of elucidating the *Mishnah*. Some texts read, "for the study of the *Gemara*." The *Gemara* (from the Aramaic, meaning "learning," "completion") is a collection of explanations and discussions on the *Mishnah*. The word *Talmud* was afterwards applied to the *Mishnah* plus the *Gemara*. There is a translation of the *Talmud* in English by Rodkinson, but it is free and incomplete in parts. See Meilziner, *Introduction to the Talmud*; Bacher, art. *Talmud*, in *Jewish Encyclopedia*; *idem*, art. *Gemara*, in the *Hebrew Union College Annual* (Cincinnati, 1904); E. Deutsch, *What is the Talmud?*; Darmsteter, *The Talmud*; Strack, *Einleitung in den Talmud*, pp. 4-5, 6 *et seq.*, 99 *et seq.*, 113 *et seq.*, 132 *et seq.*; Schechter, *On the Study of the Talmud* in *Studies*, II, p. 102 *et seq.*; Herford, *Pharisaism*, pp. 53-54.

[64], at thirty for (entering into one's full) strength, at forty for understanding, at fifty for counsel, at sixty (a man attains) old age, at seventy the hoary head, at eighty (the gift of special) strength[65], at ninety, (he bends beneath) the weight of years, at a hundred he is as if he were already dead and had passed away from the world."

25. Ben Bag Bag said, "Turn it[66], and turn it over again, for everything is in it, and contemplate it, and wax grey and old over it, and stir not from it, for thou canst have no better rule than this."

26. Ben He He said, "According to the labor is the reward"[67].

Rabbi Chanania, the son of Akashia, said, "The Holy One, blessed be He, was pleased to make Israel worthy; wherefore He gave them a copious *Torah* and many commandments, as it is said, 'It pleased the Lord, for his righteousness' sake, to magnify the *Torah* and make it honorable'".

---

64. Lit., "at twenty, to pursue." This has been variously interpreted as follows: (1) for seeking a livelihood (Bartenora, Hoffmann, Strack, Singer); (2) for the pursuit of military service (cf. Num. I, 3, and Deut. XXIV, 5; *Machzor Vitri*, p. 551. Shakespeare's "Then a soldier"); (3) the age "to pursue him for his deeds," for the celestial *bet din* (tribunal) does not punish at an age less than twenty (Bartenora's second explanation; cf. Rashi on Num. XVI, 27); (4) for the pursuit of ideals (Taylor); (5) to pursue the commandments (*Siddur Korban Minchah*).
65. Cf. Ps. XC, 10.
66. The *Torah*.
67. The last two verses are ascribed by *Abot de-Rabbi Natan* to Hillel (chapter XII, ed. Schechter, p. 55). Ben Bag Bag and Ben He He were probably proselytes and disciples of Hillel. See Bacher, *ibid.*, pp. 10-12, Taylor and Hoffmann, *ad loc.*, and *Jewish Encyclopedia*, art. *Ben Bag Bag*.

CHAPTER SIX
THE ACQUISITION OF THE TORAH

[1]

All Israel have a portion in the world to come, and it is said, "And thy people shall be all righteous; they shall inherit the land for ever, the branch of my planting, the work of my hands, that I may be glorified".

The sages taught (the following) in the language of the *Mishnah*—blessed be He that made choice of them and their *Mishnah*.

1. R. Meïr[2] said, "Whosoever labors in the *Torah* for its own sake merits many things; and not only so, but the whole world is indebted to him: he is called friend, beloved, a lover of the All-present, a lover of mankind: it clothes him with meekness and reverence; it fits him to become just, pious, upright, and faithful; it keeps him far from sin, and brings him near to virtue; through him are enjoyed counsel and sound knowledge, understanding and strength, as it is said, 'Counsel

---

1. See Introduction.
2. Chapter III, n. 32.

is mind, and sound knowledge; I am understanding; I have strength'[3]. It gives him sovereignty and dominion and discerning judgment; to him the secrets of the *Torah* are revealed; he is made like a never-failing spring and like a river that flows on with ever-increasing vigor; he becomes modest, long-suffering, and forgiving of insults; and it magnifies and exalts him above all things."

2. R. Joshua, the son of Levi[4], said, "Every day a *bat-kol*[5] goes forth from Mount Horeb, proclaiming and saying, 'Woe to mankind for contempt of the *Torah*, for whoever does not occupy himself in the *Torah* is said to be under the divine censure, as it is said, 'As a ring of gold in a swine's snout, so is a fair woman who turneth aside from discretion'[6] ; and it says, 'And the tables were the work of God, and the writing was the writing of God, graven upon the tables'[7]. Read not *charut*[8], but *cherut*[9], for no man is free but he who occupies himself in the learning of *Torah*. But whosoever labors in the *torah*,

---

3. Prov. VIII, 14. Wisdom, representing the *Torah*, utters these words.
4. R. Joshua lived about the middle of the third century.
5. *Bat kol* (lit., "daughter of a voice" or "daughter-voice"), "a small voice," "sound," "resonance," not "echo," as it is often translated. The expression *bat kol* was used in place of the longer one *bat kol min ha-shamayim*, which is "a heavenly or divine voice which proclaims God's will or judgment, His deeds, and His commandments to individuals or to number of persons, to rulers, countries, and even to whole nations." This celestial voice was a means of divine revelation lower than that of prophecy. According to Schechter, it has two peculiar features: first, its messages are reproductions of verses or sentences from the Old Testament or from the Apocrypha, and secondly, "it is audible only to those who are prepared to hear it." See Weber, *Altsynag. Theol.*, pp. 187-189; Low, *Gesammelte Schriften*, II, p. 58, n. 1; Kitto's *Cyclopedia of Biblical Lit.*, art. *Bath Kil*, and Ludwig Blau, art. *Bat Kol*, in *Jewish Encyclopedia*.
6. Proberbs XI, 22. The word נזף "censured," "placed under ban," by a form of Rabbinical interpretation known as *notarikon* (stenographer's method, abbreviation) See art. *Notarikon*, in the *Jewish Encyclopedia*, and Strack, *Einleitung*, p. 1
7. Ex. XXXII, 16.
8. Graven. The phrase "do not read ... but" followed by a suggested reading different from the original, does not mean that the Rabbis offered an emendation of the biblical text. It was merely a change of the text for homiletical purposes. See Bacher, *Die alteste Terminologie der judischen Schriftauslegung*, p. 175 *et seq.*; Friedlander, *Jewish Religion*, p. 204, and Talmudical dictionaries, *s.v.*
9. Freedom.

behold he shall be exalted, as it is said, 'And from *Mattanah* to *Nachaliel*, and from *Nachaliel* to *Bamot*'"[10].

3. He who learns from his companion a single chapter, a single rule, a single verse, a single expression, or even a single letter, ought to pay him honor, for so we find with David, King of Israel, who learned only two things from Ahitophel[11], and yet regarded him as his master, his guide, and familiar friend, as it is said, "But it was thou, a man, mine equal, my guide, and my familiar friend"[12]. Now, is it not an argument from minor to major[13], that if David, the King of Israel, who learned only two things from Ahitophel, regarded him as his master, guide, and familiar friend, he who learns from his fellow a chapter, rule, verse, expression, or even a single letter, is bound to pay him honor. And "honor" is nothing but *Torah*, as it is said, "The wise shall inherit honor[14] and the perfect shall inherit good"[15]. And "good" is nothing but *Torah*, as it is said, "For I give you good doctrine, forsake ye not my *Torah*"[16].

4. This is the way that is becoming for the study of the *Torah*: a morsel of bread with salt thou must eat[17], "and water by measure thou must drink"[18], thou must sleep upon the ground, and live a life of trouble the while thou toilest in the *Torah*. If thou doest thus,

---

10. Num. XXI, 19 *Mattanah*, "gift"; *Nachaliel*, "the heritage of God"; *Bamot*, "high places." The names of these three encampments of the Israelites in the wilderness are interpreted according to their literal meanings.
11. Ahitophel deserted David to take up the cause of his rebellious son, Absalom. See II Sam. XVI, 15; XVII, 1 *et seq.*
12. See Ps. LV, 14. The two things David learned are hinted at in Ps. LV, 15.
13. See chapter I, n. 17.
14. Prov. III, 35.
15. *Ibid.*, XXVIII, 10.
16. *Ibid.*, IV, 2.
17. Even he who has only bread and salt to eat must busy himself with the study of the *Torah*.
18. Ezek. IV, 11.

"Happy shalt thou be, and it shall be well with thee"[19], "happy shalt thou be" in this world, and "it shall be well with thee" in the world to come[20].

5. Seek not greatness for thyself, and court not honor; let thy works exceed thy learning; and crave not after the table of kings; for thy table is greater than theirs, and thy crown is greater than theirs, and thy Employer is faithful to pay thee the reward of thy work.

6. The *Torah* is greater than the priesthood and than royalty, for royalty demands thirty qualifications[21], the priesthood twenty-four[22], while the *Torah* is acquired by forty-eight. And these are they: by audible study; by a listening ear[23]; by distinct pronunciation; by understanding[24] and discernment of the heart; by awe, reverence, meekness, cheerfulness[25]; by ministering to the sages, by attaching one's self to colleagues, by discussion with disciples; by sedateness; by knowledge of the Scripture and of the *Mishnah*; by moderation in business, in intercourse with the world, in pleasure, in sleep, in conversation, in laughter; by long suffering; by a good heart; by faith in the wise; by resignation under chastisement; by recognizing one's place, rejoicing in one's portion, putting a fence to one's words, claiming no merit for one's self, by being beloved, loving the All-present, loving mankind, loving just courses, rectitude, and reproof; by keeping one's self far from honor, not boasting of one's learning, nor delighting in giving decisions; by bearing the yoke with one's fellow, judging him favorably, and leading him to truth and peace; by

---

19. Ps. CXXVIII, 2.
20. Cf. chapter IV, 1.
21. See *Sanhedrin* II, 2-5.
22. See *Baba Kamma*, 110b, etc.
23. Singer, combining the first two, reads "by audible study."
24. Taylor omits "understanding and."
25. Taylor and Hoffmann add "by purity" (בטהרה).

being composed in one's study; by asking and answering, hearing and adding thereto; by learning with the object of teaching, and by learning with the object of practising; by making one's master wise, fixing attention upon his discourse, and reporting a thing in the name of who said it. So thou hast learned, "Whosoever reports a thing in the name of him that said it brings deliverance into the world," as it is said, "And Esther told the king in the name of Mordecai"[26].

7. Great is the *Torah*, which gives life to those that practise it in this world and in the world to come, as it is said, "For they are life unto those that find them, and health to all their flesh"[27]; and it says, "It shall be health to thy navel, and marrow to thy bones"[28]; and it says, "It is a tree of life to them that grasp it, and of them that uphold it every one is rendered happy"[29]; and it says, "For they shall be a chaplet of grace unto thy head, and chains about thy neck"[30]; and it says, "It shall give to thine head a chaplet of grace, a crown of glory it shall deliver to thee"[31]; and it says, "For by me thy days shall be multiplied, and the years of thy life shall be increased"[32]; and it says, "Length of days is in its right hand; in its left hand are riches and honor"[33]; and it says, "For length of days, and years of life, and peace shall they add to thee"[34].

8. R. Simeon, the son of Judah, in the name of R. Simeon, the son of Yohai, said, "Beauty, strength, riches, honor, wisdom, old age, a

---

26. Esth. II, 22.
27. Prov. IV, 22.
28. *Ibid.*, III, 8.
29. Prov. III, 18.
30. *Ibid.*, I, 9.
31. *Ibid*, IV, 9.
32. Prov. IX, 11.
33. *Ibid.*, III, 16.
34. *Ibid.*, III, 2.

hoary head, and children are comely to the righteous and comely to the world, as it is said, 'The hoary head is a crown of glory, if it be found in the way of righteousness'[35]; and it says, 'The glory of young men is their strength, and the adornment of old men is the hoary head'[36]; and it says, 'A crown unto the wise is their riches'[37]; and it says, 'Children's children are the crown of old men, and the adornment of children are their fathers'[38]; and it is said, 'Then the moon shall be confounded and the sun ashamed; for the Lord of hosts shall reign in Mount Zion and in Jerusalem, and before his elders shall be glory'"[39]. R. Simeon, the son of Menasya, said, "These seven qualifications which the sages enumerated as becoming to the righteous were all realized in Rabbi Judah, the Prince[40], and in his sons."

9. R. Jose, the son of Kisma[41], said, "I was once walking by the way, when a man met me and saluted me, and I returned the salutation. He said to me, 'Rabbi, from what place art thou?' I said to him, 'I come from a great city of sages and scribes.' He said to me, 'If thou art willing to dwell with us in our place, I will give thee a thousand thousand golden dinars and precious stones and pearls.' I said to him, 'Wert thou to give me all the silver and gold and precious stones and pearls in the world, I would not dwell anywhere but in a home of the *Torah*'; and thus it is written in the book of Psalms by the hands of David, King of Israel, 'The law of thy mouth is better unto me than thousands of gold and silver'[42]; and not only so, but in the hour of man's departure neither silver nor gold nor precious stones nor pearls accompany him, but only *Torah* and good works, as it is said, 'When thou walkest it shall lead thee; when thou liest down it shall

---

35. *Ibid.*, XVI, 31.
36. *Ibid.*, XX, 29.
37. Prov. XIV, 24.
38. *Ibid.*, XVII, 6.
39. Isa. XXIV, 23.
40. See chapter II, n. 1.
41. He lived about 120 C.E.
42. Ps. XCIX, 72.

watch over thee; and when thou awakest it shall talk with thee'[43]; 'when thou walkest it shall lead thee'—in this world; and 'when thou awakest it shall talk with thee'—in the world to come. And it says, 'The silver is mine, and the gold is mine, saith the Lord of hosts'"[44].

10. Five possessions the Holy One, blessed be He, made especially His own in His world, and these are they, the *Torah*, heaven and earth, Abraham, Israel, and the house of the sanctuary. Whence know we this of the *Torah*? Because it is written, "The Lord possessed me as the beginning of his way, before his works, from of old"[45]. Whence of heaven and earth? Because it is written, "Thus saith the Lord, the heaven is my throne, and the earth is my footstool: what manner of house will ye build unto me? and what manner of place for my rest?"[46]; and it says, "How manifold are thy works, O Lord! In wisdom hast thou made them all: the earth is full of thy possessions"[47]. Whence of Abraham? Because it is written, "And he blessed him, and said, 'Blessed be Abram of the Most High God, possessor of heaven and earth"[48]. Whence of Israel? Because it is written, "Till thy people pass over, O Lord, till the people pass over which thou hast acquired"[49]; and it says, "As for the saints that are in the earth, they are the noble ones in whom is all my delight"[50]. Whence of the house of the sanctuary? Because it is written, "The place, O Lord, which thou hast made for Thee to dwell in, the sanctuary, O Lord, which Thy hands have prepared"[51]; and it says, "And he brought them to

---

43. Prov. VI, 22.
44. Hag. II, 8.
45. Prov. VIII, 22.
46. Isa. LXVI, 1.
47. Ps. CIV, 24.
48. Gen. XIV, 16.
49. Ex. XV, 16.
50. Ps. XVI, 3.
51. Ex. XV, 17.

the border of his sanctuary, to this mountain which his right hand had acquired"⁵².

11. Whatsoever the Holy One, blessed be He, created in His world He created but for His glory, as it is said, "Everything that is called by my name, it is for my glory I have created it, I have formed it, yea, I have made it"⁵³; and it says, "The Lord shall reign for ever and ever"⁵⁴.

Rabbi Chanania⁵⁵ , the son of Akashia, said, "The Holy One, blessed be He, was pleased to make Israel worthy; wherefore He gave them a copious *Torah* and many commandments, as it is said, 'It pleased the Lord, for his righteousness' sake, to magnify the *Torah* and make it honorable'"⁵⁶.

---

52. Ps. LXXVIII, 54.
53. Isa. XLIII, 7.
54. Ex. XV, 18.
55. The original text included the phrase "Rabbi Chanania," etc., on page 38, as the closing lines of the chapter, with the page numbers indicating the conclusion of Chapter I. Rather than referencing these sentences in the same way, this version places them directly in their intended locations within the text. The editor believes this approach more effectively preserves the essence of the original material.
56. Isaiah, xlii, 21.

Copyright © 2024 by Alicia ÉDITIONS

Credits: www.canva.com ; Alicia Éditions

ISBN EBOOK: 9782384554485

ISBN PAPERBACK: 9782384554492

ISBN HARDCOVER: 9782384554508

All rights reserved.

www.ingramcontent.com/pod-product-compliance
Lightning Source LLC
LaVergne TN
LVHW032014070526
838202LV00059B/6445